World War II: Essential Histories

World War II

The Pacific

Robert O'Neill, Series Editor; and David Horner

ROSEN
PUBLISHING®

New York

This edition published in 2010 by:

The Rosen Publishing Group, Inc.
29 East 21st Street
New York, NY 10010

Additional end matter copyright © 2010 by The Rosen Publishing Group, Inc.

Library of Congress Cataloging-in-Publication Data

Horner, D. M. (David Murray), 1948–
World War II. The Pacific / David Horner.
    p. cm.—(World War II: Essential histories)
"Robert O'Neill, series editor."
Originally published as v. 1 in The Second World War. Oxford: Osprey, 2002–2003.
Includes bibliographical references and index.
ISBN 978-1-4358-9133-3 (library binding)
1. World War, 1939–1945—Campaigns—Pacific Area—Juvenile literature. I. O'Neill, Robert John.
II. Second World War. III. Title. IV. Title: World War Two.
D767. H596 2010
940.54'26—dc22

2009029112

Manufactured in Malaysia

CPSIA Compliance Information: Batch #TW10YA: For Further Information contact Rosen Publishing, New York, New York at 1-800-237-9932

Copyright © 2002 Osprey Publishing Limited. First published in paperback by Osprey Publishing Limited.

On the cover: U.S. Marine Raiders gathered in front of a Japanese dugout on Cape Totkina on
Bougainville, Soloman Islands, which they helped to take. January 1944. *(NARA, 80-G-205686)*

Contents

Introduction

The Pacific War, the most significant event in the modern history of the Asia-Pacific region, was both a part of World War II and a distinct entity within it. Of the Axis powers – Japan, Germany, and Italy – Japan played the overwhelmingly major role in the Pacific: Germany and Italy were barely involved. By contrast, all the principal Allies – the United States, Britain, China, Australia, and the Netherlands – were deeply engaged, and the Soviet Union joined the war near its end. At the highest level, the Allies saw World War II as one conflict, in which the Pacific was just one theater. But although the Allied strategic planners had to juggle resources between theaters, the story of the Pacific War can be told separately, with the war against Germany appearing only as noises off-stage.

The Pacific War began on December 7 and 8, 1941, when Japan attacked Pearl Harbor, Malaya (a collection of states on the Malay peninsula now known as Malaysia), and the Philippines, thereby initiating a war against the USA and Britain. Japan claimed that after the USA applied crippling economic sanctions in July 1941 it had no alternative. But the war owes its origins to Japanese expansionism and militarism over a period of half a century before 1941. Japan had been at war with China since 1937, when it invaded central China, and earlier, in 1931 and 1932, Japan had seized the Chinese territory of Manchuria. While one can argue about when the war began, however, there can be no doubt about its conclusion. It ended in August 1945 when US aircraft dropped atomic bombs on Hiroshima and Nagasaki, and Japan formally surrendered in Tokyo Bay on September 2, 1945.

The war was fought over a large part of the earth's surface. Land operations stretched from the fog-bound Aleutian Islands in the northern Pacific Ocean to the steaming tropical jungles of the Solomon Islands in the South Pacific. To the east, Japanese forces seized lonely Wake Island in the mid-Pacific; to the west, they fought in the jungle hills bordering India and Burma. Naval operations were more widespread, reaching east to Hawaii, south to Sydney Harbor and west to Madagascar, off the African coast.

It was a war of daring strategic maneuvers, generally in a maritime environment. These included Japan's astonishing advances during the first six months, the key struggles around the perimeter of the so-called Greater East Asia Co-prosperity Sphere and the Allied counteroffensives. It was a war of great naval battles, such as those in the Coral Sea, at Midway, at Leyte, and in the Philippine Sea. It was also a war of grim jungle battles, such as in Guadalcanal, New Guinea, and Burma. There were bold and bloody amphibious landings, large-scale land operations (in Burma and the Philippines), savage guerrilla wars, clandestine operations, fearsome bombing attacks, and a bitter submarine campaign.

The Pacific War saw the application of new military capabilities and technologies, such as aircraft carriers, ship-borne air power, submarines, amphibious warfare, and signals intelligence. Finally, atomic bombs were used for the first time. The war was fought by some famous military commanders – Generals Douglas MacArthur, William Slim, and Yamashita Tomoyuki, and Admirals Chester Nimitz, William Halsey, and Yamamoto Isoruku.

It was an unusual war in that although Japan initiated it, it never had a chance of winning. The Japanese strategy was to seize southeast Asia and hope that the Allies would grow weary and allow them to keep at least some of their gains. After the "infamy" of Pearl Harbor, however, the USA was never going to rest until Japan was crushed, and inevitably Japan was overpowered by American industrial might.

Although Japan was crushed, it did achieve some of its aims. Its successes splintered the invincibility of European colonial power, leading eventually to independence for the former European and American colonies: Indochina, Burma, Malaya, Indonesia, and the Philippines. It also contributed to independence for India. Japan had hoped to find easy pickings in a weak and divided China; instead, China became unified under communist rule, except for the Nationalist bastion in the former Japanese colony of Taiwan. Japan lost its other colony in Korea, which became two separate but warring nations. And remarkably, Japan rose from the ashes to become an economic powerhouse.

Japan waged a pitiless war, including the massacre at Nanking, the brutal treatment and enslavement of prisoners of war, and the enforced recruitment of euphemistically called "comfort women." This left a legacy of bitterness across the whole region, but especially in China and Korea. For those whose lives were wrecked by the war, it was little consolation to learn that Japan also treated its own civilians and servicemen cruelly. As usual, the burden of war fell heaviest on the ordinary people, with millions of deaths in Japan, China, India, and southeast Asia.

The Pacific War therefore completely reshaped political entities in Asia and changed national attitudes. Although more than half a century has passed since the end of the war, an understanding of it is still crucial if one is to appreciate the problems faced by the dynamic area now known as the Asia-Pacific.

Note: Spellings of places and people in this book are those used at the time.

Chronology

1931–32 Japan establishes puppet state
of Manchukuo

1933 **March 25** Japan leaves League
of Nations

1936 **November 25** Japan signs
Anti-Comintern Pact with Germany

1937 **July 7** Beginning of general attack by
Japanese forces on China
(China Incident)
August 13 Fighting begins between
Japanese and Chinese troops
at Shanghai

1939 **July 2** Japanese forces in Manchukuo
cross into Outer Mongolia
(Nomonhan Incident)
September 16 Cease-fire with Soviet
forces in Manchukuo

1940 **July 17** Burma Road closed for
three months
September 22 Japan granted bases
in Indochina
September 27 Tripartite Pact
between Germany, Italy, and Japan

1941 **July 24** Japanese troops land in
southern Indochina
July 26 American government freezes
Japanese assets in the USA; General
MacArthur appointed to command
US army in Far East
July 27 Japanese troops start
occupying French Indochina
October 17 General Tojo becomes
Prime Minister of Japan
December 7–8 Japanese attack
Malaya, Pearl Harbor, and
the Philippines
December 10 *Prince of Wales* and

Repulse sunk; main Japanese landing
in the Philippines
December 14 Japanese start invasion
of Burma
December 17 Japanese land in
British Borneo
December 24 Wake Island captured
by Japanese
December 26 Surrender of
Hong Kong

1942 **January 23** Japanese forces
attack Rabaul
January 30 Japanese forces
attack Ambon
January 31 Defending forces in
Malaya withdraw to Singapore Island
February 15 Singapore
Island surrenders
February 19 Japanese bomb Darwin
February 19–20 Japanese forces land
on Timor
February 27 Naval battle of Java Sea
February 28 Japanese forces land
in Java
March 8 Japanese troops enter
Rangoon; Japanese land in New Guinea
March 17 MacArthur appointed to
command Southwest Pacific Area
April 5 Japanese carrier-borne aircraft
attack Colombo
April 9 American forces on
Bataan surrender
April 18 Doolittle raid on Tokyo
May 5–8 Battle of the Coral Sea
May 6 American forces on
Corregidor surrender
May 20 Allied forces withdraw
from Burma
May 31 Attack on Sydney Harbor
June 4–6 Battle of Midway Island
June 7 Japanese land in
Aleutian Islands

July 21 Japanese land at Gona area, Papua
August 7 Americans land in Solomons
August 8–9 Naval battle of Savo Island
August 25–26 Japanese land at Milne Bay
September 17 Japanese drive over Owen Stanley Range halted at Imita Ridge
November 12–15 Naval battle of Guadalcanal

1943   **January 23** Organized Japanese resistance in Papua ends
February 7 Last Japanese withdraw from Guadalcanal
February 13 First Chindit operation into Burma
March 2–4 Battle of the Bismarck Sea
April 18 Death of Admiral Yamamoto
May 11 American forces land on Attu in Aleutian Islands
June 30 Americans land on New Georgia
August 1 Japanese declare Burma independent
September 4 Australians land near Lae, New Guinea
September 16 Australian divisions enter Lae
October 7 Mountbatten takes command of Southeast Asia Command
October 14 Japanese declare independence of the Philippines
November 1 American troops land on Bougainville, northern Solomons
November 20 American forces invade Makin and Tarawa in Gilberts
December 15 Americans land on New Britain

1944   **January 9** Allied forces overrun Maungdaw on Arakan front in Burma
January 31 Americans invade Marshall Islands
February 15 New Zealand forces invade Green Island
February 29 Americans invade Admiralty Islands

March 2 Second Chindit operation launched into Burma
March 15 Japanese Imphal offensive from Burma begins
April 22 Americans land at Hollandia and Aitape
April 24 Australians enter Madang
May 27 Americans land on Biak Island
June 5 Start of Japanese withdrawal from Kohima
June 15 Americans invade Saipan in the Marianas; American strategic air offensive against Japan begins from China
June 19–20 Battle of the Philippine Sea
July 2 Americans land on Noemfoor
July 18 General Tojo falls from power as Japanese Prime Minister
July 21 Americans invade Guam
July 30 Japanese begin withdrawal from Myitkyina, Burma
September 15 Americans land in Palau Islands (Peleliu) and on Morotai in the Halmaheras
October 10 US Third Fleet attacks Okinawa
October 20 Americans land on Leyte
October 23–26 Naval battle of Leyte Gulf
November 24 Superfortresses attack Japan from bases in the Marianas

1945   **January 3** Allies occupy Akyab in Burma
January 9 American forces land on Luzon
January 22 Burma Road reopened
February 19 American forces land on Iwo Jima
March 9 Japanese seize control in French Indochina
March 9–10 First fire-bomb attack on Tokyo
March 10 American forces land on Mindanao
March 20 British capture Mandalay
April 1 American forces land on Okinawa
May 1 Australians invade Tarakan
May 3 British troops capture Rangoon

June 10 Australians land at Brunei Bay
July 1 Australians land at Balikpapan
August 7 Atomic bomb dropped
on Hiroshima
August 9 Atomic bomb dropped on
Nagasaki; Soviet troops
invade Manchukuo
August 14 Emperor Hirohito
announces Japanese forces'
unconditional surrender
August 15 VJ-Day; all offensive
action against Japan comes to an end
August 17 Sukarno announces
Indonesia to be independent
September 2 Japanese sign
instrument of surrender in Tokyo Bay

The expansion of imperial Japan, 1891–1941

The Pacific War was caused by the expansionist ambitions of Imperial Japan and the train of events that led to it can be described fairly easily. It is much harder to explain why Japan initiated a war against the one country that had the power to crush it – the USA. The answer is perhaps found in Japan's unique culture and history. Having not experienced defeat for a thousand years, and believing in the superiority of their race, culture, and spirit, the Japanese could not conceive of defeat. Somehow, trusting in the living-god Emperor, they would win, even if many would die in the process.

The origins of the war therefore lie in Japan's emergence after more than two centuries of isolation from the outside world. To protect itself from foreign influences, in the early seventeenth century Japan had expelled all foreigners and had severely restricted foreign access. This isolation was shattered in 1853, when four American warships appeared in Tokyo Bay and their commander, Commodore Matthew Perry, began negotiations that led eventually to a commercial treaty between the USA and Japan.

Thereafter the Japanese moved rapidly to modernize their country. The power of the feudal warlords collapsed and in 1868 the new Emperor announced a policy of seeking knowledge from around the world. Japan adopted a vaguely democratic constitution with an elected parliament, or Diet. Compulsory education was introduced, although with heavy emphasis on obedience to the Emperor. Asked by their teachers about their "dearest ambition," schoolboys would answer, "To die for the Emperor." The Japanese craved European technology and expertise, but did not have the time or the inclination to absorb Western ideas of democracy or liberalism.

Japanese insecurity and expansionism

The Japanese were acutely conscious of their vulnerability. Over the preceding centuries, European powers had seized colonies in the Asia-Pacific area. Britain held Malaya, Burma, and India, the French were in Indochina, the Dutch owned the East Indies (now Indonesia), and Germany had part of New Guinea. The Europeans and the Americans had also won concessions from a weak and disorganized China. If Japan were to survive, it had to establish a powerful and modern army and a capable navy, and to support these forces it had to begin a rapid process of industrialization. Lacking natural resources but possessing a large, industrious population, Japan had to secure supplies of raw materials and find markets for its goods.

The Japanese observed that the European powers had gained economically by exploiting their military and diplomatic power in Asia. Taking this lead, in 1894 Japan initiated a short and successful war with China over access to Korea, and the following year China ceded Formosa (Taiwan) and the Liaotung peninsula in southern Manchuria, which included the fine harbor of Port Arthur. Under pressure from Russia, Germany, and France, Japan was forced to withdraw from Manchuria. Russia moved into Manchuria, while Germany and France grabbed further concessions in China. To the enraged Japanese, it seemed that there was one rule for the European powers and a different rule for Asian countries. Three years later the USA took control of the Philippines.

The Japanese were determined to gain control of those areas that they saw as vital to their economic survival. In 1904 Japan blockaded Port Arthur, and moved troops into Korea and Manchuria. In a bloody war with heavy casualties on both sides, the Japanese defeated the Russian army in Manchuria and destroyed the Russian fleet sent to relieve Port Arthur. For the first time, an Asian power had defeated a European power, and the Japanese army gained in prestige and power. Japan took control of the Liaotung peninsula and stationed troops to protect the Manchurian railroad. By 1910, Japan had annexed Korea.

Japan obtained tremendous advantages from World War I. As one of the Allies, it seized Germany's possessions in China and the Pacific, but never sent land forces to Europe. Fueled by the demands of the war, Japanese industries continued to expand and Japan built up its merchant navy.

In the postwar settlement, Japan retained the former German Pacific colonies under a mandate from the League of Nations, but was upset by the Allies' refusal to endorse a statement about nonracial discrimination. Japan was thus confirmed as a principal power in the Pacific, but was viewed with suspicion by both the USA and Britain. At a conference in Washington in 1921–22, the USA, Britain, and Japan agreed to limit their capital ships according to a ratio of 5:5:3, and the USA and Britain undertook not to fortify their Pacific possessions. Japan was aggrieved at apparent restrictions to its navy, but as both Britain and the USA also deployed their forces in the Atlantic, Japan was left as the most powerful navy in the western Pacific. Still suspicious of Japan, in 1923 Britain decided to establish a naval base at Singapore, to which it would send its main fleet in time of crisis in the Pacific.

Meanwhile, the Japanese economy and society were coming under great strain. During the 1920s numerous earthquakes – the largest striking Tokyo in 1923 – shattered cities and factories. As the world economic system began to falter, Western countries applied trade restrictions that hurt Japanese industries. The Great Depression is generally thought to have begun with the Wall Street crash in 1929, but by 1926 more than

The Japanese Emperor, Hirohito, came to the throne in 1926, aged 25. He had traveled in Europe and was an amateur marine biologist of repute. He exercised little power, but historical debate still continues over whether he encouraged the militarists. A Japanese nationalist, he seemed fatalistically to accept the inevitability of war. (AKG Berlin)

three million Japanese industrial workers had lost their jobs. The Japanese government came under increasing pressure from militant nationalistic groups, often led by young army officers. This was a similar environment to that which led to the rise of Nazism in Germany, fascism in Italy, and communism in various countries. In Japan a homegrown militarism built on the Japanese people's belief in their national uniqueness and their heaven-granted mandate to assume leadership in east Asia.

In Manchuria and northern China, Japan was facing new challenges. The Soviet Union was likely to oppose Japanese ambitions in the Far East. And in China, nationalist forces were being consolidated under Chiang Kai-shek. Fiercely nationalistic Japan ignored the nationalist aspirations of other Asian countries such as China and Korea.

The Japanese semiautonomous Kwantung Army, policing the Manchurian railroad, was a highly political organization that attracted the best and most ambitious Japanese officers and dominated commercial development in the ostensibly Chinese province. On September 18, 1931, officers of the Kwantung Army falsely accused the Chinese of sabotaging the Port Arthur–Mukden railroad. Against the wishes of both the Japanese government and the commander of the Kwantung Army, Japanese forces attacked the numerically stronger armies of the local Chinese warlords and quickly overran Manchuria. Powerless, the Japanese government acquiesced, and the following year Japan established a puppet state – Manchukuo – nominally ruled by Emperor Pu Yi, but actually controlled by the Japanese commander of the Kwantung Army. In 1932 the Japanese seized the nearby province of Jehol and added eastern Chahar in 1935. Manchukuo had a population of 34 million, of whom 240,000 were Japanese (increasing to 837,000 in 1939).

This so-called Manchurian Incident marked the beginning of full-scale Japanese aggression in Asia. The US Secretary of State condemned Japan, and after an investigation the League of Nations branded Japan as the aggressor. In response, in March 1933 Japan withdrew from the League of Nations. The Japanese War Minister, General Araki Sadao, complained that the League of Nations did not respect Japan's "holy mission" to establish peace in the Orient, but vowed that the day would come when "we will make the world look up to our national virtues."

Despite these belligerent statements, the Japanese government was actually in disarray – what one commentator described as "government by assassination." In November 1930 the Japanese Prime Minister was gunned down for accepting allegedly humiliating conditions at a naval conference in London. In February 1932 two leading politicians were assassinated by members of the Blood Brotherhood – modern-day samurai warriors

who were prepared to sacrifice themselves for the good of Japan. In May 1932 they murdered the Prime Minister for criticizing Japanese aggression in Manchuria. The assassins, described by War Minister Araki as "irrepressible patriots," received jail terms that were later commuted.

In February 1936 radical army officers attempted a *coup d'état*, murdering several leading government ministers. The coup attempt failed, but the army gained even more power. In 1937 the War Minister (a serving army officer) submitted a bill to parliament to give the government absolute control over industry, labor, and the press. The Diet meekly voted its approval. Also the government initiated a plan to expand its heavy industries to enable it to wage a total war for three years, and it stepped up the naval building program. In November 1936 the army had negotiated the Anti-Comintern Pact with Germany and Italy. It was directed squarely against the Soviet Union, which was supporting China.

The Sino-Japanese War

On the night of July 7, 1937, shots were fired at a Japanese detachment on maneuvers a few miles from Peking (modern-day Beijing). Japanese and Chinese forces had engaged in frequent skirmishes during the previous six years, but this time the Nationalist Chinese leader, Chiang Kai-shek, believed that he could no longer tolerate Japanese provocation. To some historians the "China Incident," as the Japanese called it, marks the true beginning of World War II. China and Japan were to remain at war until 1945.

On August 14, 1937, Nationalist Chinese planes struck Japanese warships at Shanghai. The Japanese deployed 10 divisions to north China and five to Shanghai. When, in October, President Franklin D. Roosevelt finally condemned Japan's aggression, a leading Japanese, Matsuoka Yosuke, soon to be Foreign Minister, retorted: "Japan is expanding and what country in its expansion era has ever failed to be trying to its neighbors?" In November the Japanese

Japanese troops in a victory pose at a captured Chinese artillery camp, Shanghai, November 1937. From August to early November the Chinese resisted Japanese attempts to take the city. After it fell, the Japanese moved quickly and secured Nanking on December 13. (AKG Berlin)

army drove the Chinese out of Shanghai and next month took the Nationalist capital, Nanking, where it engaged in an orgy of killing, rape, and looting. More than a quarter of a million civilians were slaughtered.

Contemptuous of Western public opinion, Japanese planes and shore batteries sank an American gunboat, USS *Panay*, which was evacuating diplomatic staffs from Nanking, and the American government chose to accept a Japanese apology. Nonetheless, Western observers in China, many of them American missionaries, publicized stories of Japanese atrocities, and the American government gradually sought ways to assist the Nationalist Chinese.

Thrusting deeper into China, by the end of 1938 Japan had captured large areas of northern China, the Yangtze valley, and pockets along the coast. Chiang Kai-shek withdrew his government to the inland city of Chungking and tried to come to a cooperative arrangement with the Chinese Communists under Mao Tse-tung. The Communists conducted guerrilla warfare against the Japanese, who had established a puppet Chinese government in their area of occupation. Meanwhile, the Nationalist Chinese were working hard to win American support.

The Japanese now faced a dilemma. They could not conquer all of China, but the war was a heavy drain on their resources, fuel, and finances. Japanese army leaders hoped to resolve the war in China so that they could deal with their principal enemy, the Soviet Union. But to conclude the war, Japan needed fuel and other resources from southeast Asia. If Western countries would not supply this fuel then Japan would have to seize it. The Japanese navy leaders realized that expansion to the south would bring war, with the USA as their principal enemy. Japan now stepped up preparations for a major war.

Japanese soldiers entering Nanking in December 1937. Japanese commanders unleashed days of wanton slaughter in the city, the notorious Rape of Nanking. (AKG Berlin)

Towards the end of 1938 the Japanese Prime Minister, Prince Konoye Fumimaro, spelled out Japan's plans for a New Order for East Asia, involving the eradication of European and American imperialism and also of communism from east Asia. Later the Japanese would declare their national objective to be the setting up of a Greater East Asia Co-prosperity Sphere. In effect, the Asian countries would be subservient to Japan, providing it with raw materials and markets.

Meanwhile, Soviet support for the Chinese precipitated several clashes between the Kwantung Army and Soviet forces. Finally, in July 1939 the Kwantung Army crossed into Mongolia. A Soviet army mounted a counteroffensive near Nomonhan that killed more than 18,000 Japanese troops. In the midst of this campaign, the Japanese were shocked to learn of the Nazi–Soviet Pact. They quickly arranged a cease-fire in Manchuria.

Japan looks south

Bogged down in China and checked by the Soviet Union, the Japanese were unsure of their next step. Then, in September 1939 Germany invaded Poland, and Britain and France declared war on Germany. The German invasion of France in May 1940 suddenly offered Japan new opportunities to cut China's overseas supplies. Chased out of Europe and hammered from the air, Britain was not strong enough to resist Japan's demand in July 1940 to close the road from Rangoon in Burma to Chungking, which was supplying the Nationalist government with vital supplies. Nor could the Vichy French government, formed after the German

The Japanese War Minister, General Tojo Hideki (center, with mustache), and the Foreign Minister, Matsuoka Yosuke (fourth from right), join German and Italian officials to toast the Tripartite Pact signed between the three countries in September 1940. The Pact recognized the leadership of Japan in establishing a new order in Greater East Asia. A "none-too-intelligent professional soldier," Tojo became Prime Minister in October 1941 and took Japan into the war. Later, with the additional portfolio of Home Minister, Tojo, known as "the Razor," directed the arrest of his political opponents. (Australian War Memorial)

occupation, resist demands to close the port of Haiphong and to give access to bases in northern Vietnam from which Japanese planes could attack southern China.

But the German occupation of France also spurred the Americans into action. In May 1940 the Americans decided to station their Pacific Fleet at Hawaii and the following month they began a large naval expansion program so that their navy could operate in both the Atlantic and Pacific oceans. In September the US Congress agreed to a peacetime draft, and in December it made $100 million in credit available to the Chinese Nationalist government. The Japanese imperial navy reacted by ordering a full mobilization – a process that would be completed by December 1941.

Thus, by the second half of 1940, war between Japan, the USA, and Britain had become increasingly likely. Britain, the USA (concerned for the security of the Philippines), Australia, and the Netherlands considered defensive plans in southeast Asia. Belatedly, Britain built up its garrison in Malaya and Singapore with British, Indian, and Australian troops. But preoccupied by events in Europe and the Middle East, Britain did not give the defense of Malaya high priority.

The German attack on Russia on June 22, 1941, fundamentally changed the situation. Japan could either fall on Russia's Far East empire while Russia was fighting for its life in Europe or it could continue its southern expansion secure in the knowledge that Russia would be too preoccupied to attack in Manchuria. In April, Japan had signed a nonaggression pact with the Soviet Union. On July 2, Japan decided to strike south.

The expansion of Japan 1920–1941

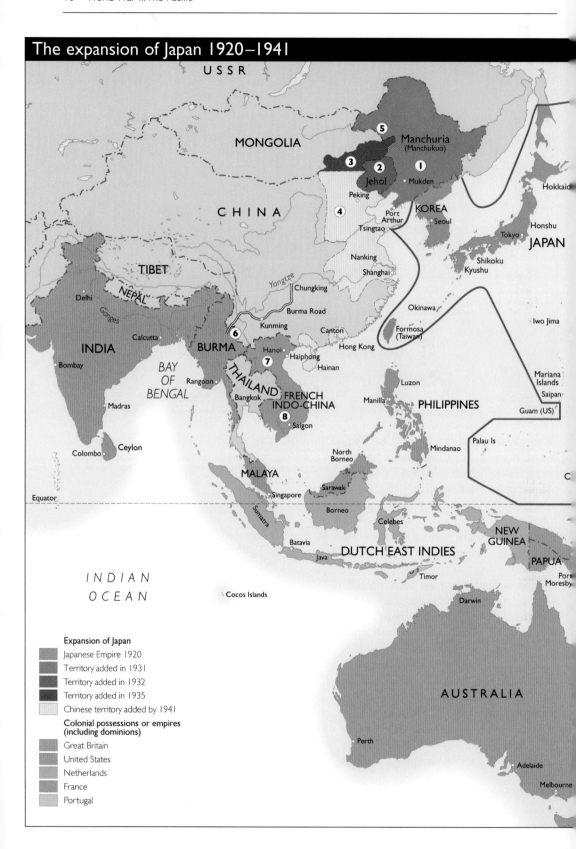

USSR

MONGOLIA

Manchuria
(Manchukuo)

⑤

③   ②   ①

Jehol   Mukden

Peking

CHINA

KOREA

Port
Arthur   Seoul

Tsingtao

④

Nanking

Shanghai

Chungking

Yangtze

Burma Road

Kunming   Canton

TIBET

NEPAL

Delhi

Ganges

Calcutta

INDIA   BURMA   ⑥

Hanoi

Bombay   Haiphong

THAILAND   ⑦   Hainan

BAY
OF
BENGAL   Rangoon

Bangkok   FRENCH
INDO-CHINA

Madras   ⑧   Saigon

Colombo   Ceylon

Hokkaid

Honshu

Tokyo

JAPAN

Shikoku
Kyushu

Okinawa

Formosa
(Taiwan)

Hong Kong

Iwo Jima

Luzon

Manila   PHILIPPINES

Mariana
Islands

Saipan

Guam (US)

Mindanao   Palau Is

North
Borneo

MALAYA

Singapore   Sarawak

Sumatra   Borneo

Celebes

Batavia   DUTCH EAST INDIES

Java   Timor

NEW
GUINEA

PAPUA

Por
Moresby

Equator

INDIAN
OCEAN   Cocos Islands

Darwin

AUSTRALIA

Perth

Adelaide

Melbourne

Expansion of Japan

Japanese Empire 1920

Territory added in 1931

Territory added in 1932

Territory added in 1935

Chinese territory added by 1941

**Colonial possessions or empires
(including dominions)**

Great Britain

United States

Netherlands

France

Portugal

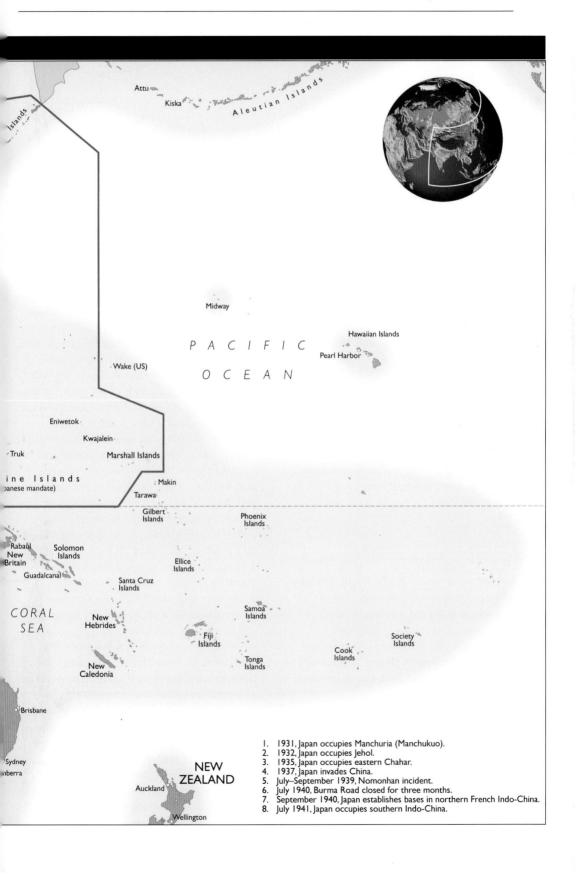

Attu
Kiska
Aleutian Islands

Midway

PACIFIC

OCEAN

Hawaiian Islands
Pearl Harbor

Wake (US)

Eniwetok
Kwajalein
Truk
Marshall Islands

ine Islands
(Japanese mandate)

Makin
Tarawa

Gilbert
Islands

Phoenix
Islands

Rabaul
New
Britain
Solomon
Islands
Guadalcanal

Ellice
Islands

Santa Cruz
Islands

CORAL
SEA
New
Hebrides

Samoa
Islands

Society
Islands

Fiji
Islands

Cook
Islands

New
Caledonia

Tonga
Islands

Brisbane

Sydney
nberra

NEW
ZEALAND
Auckland

Wellington

1. 1931, Japan occupies Manchuria (Manchukuo).
2. 1932, Japan occupies Jehol.
3. 1935, Japan occupies eastern Chahar.
4. 1937, Japan invades China.
5. July–September 1939, Nomonhan incident.
6. July 1940, Burma Road closed for three months.
7. September 1940, Japan establishes bases in northern French Indo-China.
8. July 1941, Japan occupies southern Indo-China.

Powerful Japan faced certain defeat

Any comparison of the military and industrial strengths of the Japanese Empire and the Allies must conclude that Japan had no chance of winning. While Japan could deploy more than a million soldiers, three of its enemies could do likewise. And while Japan possessed the world's third largest navy, it was opposed by the even stronger American and British navies. Yet Japan began the war with considerable advantages. By seizing the initiative, it severely damaged the US Pacific Fleet at Pearl Harbor, eliminated the dangerous US bombing force in the Philippines, and threw the British forces in Malaya off-balance. Once the USA lost its western Pacific bases, it had to cross thousands of miles of ocean to take the fight to the Japanese. The USA also had to divide its forces between the European and Pacific theaters. To an even greater extent, Britain concentrated on Europe, and it could not deploy its naval strength fully until the last year of the war.

Japan's military strength

In 1937 Japan was a strong, technologically advanced nation with a population of 70 million. During the 1930s its open, market-oriented economy had been transformed into a directed war economy, but it weakness was its heavy dependence on overseas supplies of oil, raw materials, and rice.

By 1941 the Japanese army consisted of 31 divisions, with a further 13 in the Kwantung Army. Each division generally numbered about 18,000 men. By Western standards, much of the army's heavy equipment was obsolete, but the troops were well trained and experienced from years of operations in China. By the end of the war,

Japan had raised 170 infantry, 13 air, four tanks, and four anti-aircraft divisions in a force numbering 2.3 million. The lack of adequate tanks and heavy artillery was not an important factor in jungle and island warfare, although the army's defeat by Soviet forces in 1939 had revealed its inadequacy against a well-equipped enemy in open terrain.

One of the strengths of the Japanese armed forces was the Bushido code of honor – the way of the warrior. All members of the armed forces were responsible directly to the Emperor. Military instructions emphasized absolute obedience to orders and forbade retreat in any circumstances. These attitudes led to fanatical resistance, often resulting in suicidal banzai charges, with the troops shouting the battle cry, "Long live the Emperor!" Later in the war, Japanese aircraft pilots conducted suicidal kamikaze attacks on Allied ships. Another outcome was the atrocious treatment of Allied prisoners of war. But life was also hard and discipline brutal for the conscripted Japanese soldiers.

In December 1941 Japan's navy numbered 391 warships, including 10 battleships and 10 aircraft carriers. It was a well-trained force; its gunnery was good and its navigators were skillful. Some ships were new, with modern weapons – the Long Lance torpedo was exceptional – but others were older. Its strength was the naval air force, with its 1,750 fighters, torpedo bombers, and bombers, operating from both aircraft carriers and island bases.

The Japanese army's air force was based mainly in China, but units were later deployed to larger islands such as New Guinea and the Philippines. While Japan's considerable industrial capacity allowed it to construct almost 70,000 aircraft between 1941 and 1945, it was not able to sustain the constant technological improvements that marked the

The Japanese Zero – the Mitsubishi A6m2 Navy Type O carrier fighter – was one of the outstanding aircraft of the war. Armor plating and self-sealing tanks were sacrificed to give the Zero maximum speed and maneuverability. It could outperform most Allied aircraft in 1941 and was flown by well-trained and experienced pilots. (US National Archives)

Allied industrial effort. As the war progressed, the Allies had increasingly superior aircraft.

Theoretically, Japanese military operations were directed by Imperial General Headquarters (formed in 1937), but in practice, the army and navy headquarters staff operated independently. Army operations were generally controlled by the China Expeditionary, Southern Expeditionary, or Kwantung armies. Below this level were the area armies; these normally included several armies (equivalent to Western corps) and an air army. Most Japanese warships came under the Combined Fleet, headed in 1941 by Admiral Yamamoto Isoruku. This was subdivided into fleets with various compositions, such as the battleship force and the striking force.

Japan's military operations often suffered from a lack of clear strategic direction, caused by lack of cooperation between army and navy leaders. More generally, however, the Allies' main advantage lay in the industrial power of the USA.

The USA's military strength

At the outbreak of war, the American population of 141 million was about twice that of Japan, but its industrial capacity was considerably greater. For example, in 1937 the USA produced 28.8 million tons of steel, while Japan produced 5.8 million. This industrial strength and large population enabled the USA to expand its armed forces at an unprecedented rate and to manufacture huge quantities of equipment and war matériel not only for its own forces but also for Allied forces.

The USA fought a war in Europe, but still deployed massive forces in the Pacific. In early 1940 the US army numbered only 160,000, but after conscription was introduced in September 1940, it grew rapidly: in December its strength was 1.6 million; by March 1945 it had reached 8.1 million. These figures included the US Army Air Force (USAAF), which grew from 270,000 to 1.8 million in the same period. In April 1945 the US army had 5 million soldiers deployed overseas; 1.45 million of these were in the Pacific and China–Burma–India theaters. The USA also deployed 11 field armies. Two remained in the USA, six went to the European theater, and three were in the Pacific – the Sixth and Eighth in the Southwest Pacific Area, and the

Tenth at Okinawa. Each army consisted of two or more corps, and each of these had two or more divisions. During the war the US army formed 90 divisions. General George C. Marshall remained the Chief of Staff of the US army throughout the war.

Of the USAAF's 16 air forces, seven served in the Pacific and the China–Burma–India theaters. In September 1939 the USAAF had 2,470 aircraft; at its peak in July 1944, 79,908. The USA's strength was its capacity to construct aircraft – almost 300,000 during the war – and its ability to improve aircraft designs each year. Although the USAAF was theoretically part of the army, it acted as an independent service and its chief, General Hap Arnold, was one of the four members of the US Joint Chiefs of Staff.

While the US army and USAAF were divided between Europe and the Pacific, the US navy deployed the majority of its strength in the Pacific. Like the other services, it too underwent a huge expansion. In July 1940 its

Mass-produced Liberty ships under construction in an American shipyard. In 1940 Britain ordered 60 simply designed ships, described as being "built by the mile and chopped off by the yard." The following year the USA ordered 200 of these 7,126-ton, 11-knot ships (12.66 mph; 20.37 km/hr). A total of 27,103 were constructed in the USA during the war. (US National Archives)

strength was 160,997; by August 1945 it was 4.5 million. In December 1941 the Pacific Fleet, based at Pearl Harbor, included nine battleships, three carriers, 21 heavy and light cruisers, 67 destroyers, and 27 submarines. The Asiatic Fleet, based at Manila, had three cruisers, 13 destroyers, 29 submarines, two seaplane tenders, and 16 gunboats. The total force was inferior to the Japanese navy and this disparity was increased by the loss of battleships at Pearl Harbor.

However, the USA's immense shipbuilding program, begun in the late 1930s and 1940, soon changed the balance. During the war the USA constructed 88,000 landing craft, 215 submarines, 147 carriers, and 952 other warships. The aircraft carriers included large, fast-strike carriers transporting up to 90 aircraft, and numerous, smaller escort carriers with 16 to 36 aircraft. The US navy included a strong air force (it grew from 11,000 in 1940 to 430,000 in 1945) and the US Marine Corps, which deployed six divisions, all in the Pacific. Admiral Ernest King was appointed Commander-in-Chief of the US fleet in March 1942 and remained in command throughout the war.

The British Empire

By December 1941 Britain had been at war for more than two years. Its army had been forced to evacuate France in 1940 and had fought a series of debilitating campaigns in the Middle East. Its air force had defended Britain from air attacks, which were still continuing. The Royal Navy was fighting the battle of the Atlantic against German U-boats and was supporting Britain's forces in the Mediterranean. Few military resources could be spared for the Far East. The imperial troops in Malaya included two Indian divisions and an understrength Australian division, while most of the aircraft there were inferior to those of the Japanese. There were few major naval units and no aircraft carriers.

British forces in southeast Asia were always afforded a low priority for men and equipment, and operations would have been

impossible without the assistance of forces raised in India. Of the 1 million troops that later served in Southeast Asia Command (formed in August 1943), 700,000 were Indian, 100,000 were British, and about 90,000 came from British colonies in west and east Africa. The equivalent of about 17 Indian divisions served outside India during the war; of these, two served in Malaya and 11 in Burma.

Britain provided a larger proportion of the air forces. In December 1943, for example, Air Command Southeast Asia had an effective strength of 67 squadrons. Of these, 44 were from the Royal Air Force, 19 from the USAAF, two from the Royal Indian Air Force, one from the Royal Canadian Air Force, and one from the Royal Netherlands Air Force.

The British Eastern Fleet operated in the Indian Ocean but was not a strong force until 1944. In November 1943 it had one battleship, one escort carrier, seven cruisers, two armed merchant cruisers, 11 destroyers, 13 escort vessels, and six submarines. In

Indian artillery troops training in Malaya in 1941. In 1939 the Indian army included about 200,000 Indian soldiers, a further 83,000 from the princely states, and 63,000 British troops. The Indian army expanded rapidly and by the end of the war numbered 2.5 million – all volunteers. The Indian units were mostly staffed with British officers, and Indian brigades usually included a British battalion. (Imperial War Museum, London, print from MARS, Lincs)

1945 the British Pacific Fleet was formed to operate with the Americans in the Pacific. With two battleships, four carriers, five cruisers, and 14 destroyers it was the largest and most powerful British fleet of the war.

Australia and New Zealand

Before the war Australia had a minuscule regular army with about 80,000 part-time volunteers in the militia. The air force was also very small with about 160 mostly obsolete aircraft. Only the navy, with six cruisers, five old destroyers, and two sloops, was even close to being ready for battle. The army and air force expanded through voluntary enlistment and, with navy units, they operated with British forces in the Middle East and Europe. After the outbreak of war in the Pacific, most of these units returned to Australia, where they became part of the Southwest Pacific Area under General MacArthur.

By mid-1942 Australia had 11 divisions in Australia, and during 1942 and 1943 Australia provided the majority of the Allied land forces in the Southwest Pacific Area. At its largest, the army numbered 500,000 from a population of 7 million, and six divisions served on operations in the southwestern Pacific. The army was divided between the volunteers of the Australian Imperial Force, who could serve in any area, and the militia, which included conscripts and could serve only in Australia and its territories. The air force, with more than 50 squadrons, flying both American and Australian-built British aircraft, provided a useful supplement to the Allied air forces, although Australia also maintained a large contribution to the Allied strategic bombing campaign in Europe. The navy formed a strong squadron with the Allied naval forces, but had no carriers. Considering its limited population and industrial base, Australia made a substantial contribution to the Pacific War.

New Zealand made a much smaller contribution, preferring to leave its largest expeditionary division in Europe. A small New Zealand division, along with air and naval units, fought in the Solomon Islands.

China

The Chinese armed forces were divided between those under the control of the Nationalist government, those organized by the Communist Party, and those under various warlords. The Nationalist army expanded from a force of about 1.2 million in 1937 to one of 5.7 million in August 1945, organized into 300 divisions. It was composed of conscripts, who were usually treated badly. Poorly equipped and inadequately trained, the Chinese divisions had generally a low level of capability. Several Chinese divisions fought under American command in Burma, where they performed creditably. The Chinese air force was organized and flown by American volunteers. The main Communist army expanded from about 92,000 in 1937 to 910,000 in 1945. It concentrated on guerrilla warfare and on establishing good relations with peasant communities.

Conclusion

Japan, the USA, China, and India each deployed armies of more than 1 million soldiers. In addition, the Soviet Union could also deploy millions of troops. But with a few exceptions, these forces were never engaged in intense, large-scale land operations for long periods. The geographic spread of operations across the maritime areas of the Pacific meant that air and naval forces played a major role. It was here that the industrial strength of the USA gave the Allies a significant advantage. Indeed by the end of the war, the US navy in the Pacific was the largest in history. Once the Allies could apply their naval and air strength to the fullest extent, their final victory was inevitable.

The slide toward inevitable war

Internal Japanese politics played a crucial role in shaping the events that led to war in December 1941. The most fanatical member of the government was the Foreign Minister, Matsuoka, who, after Germany attacked Russia, wanted Japan also to attack Russia. He could not persuade his colleagues and on July 2, 1941 they decided to seize bases in southern Indochina. On July 16 the Japanese Prime Minister, Konoye, dropped Matsuoka from the Cabinet, but the Cabinet could still not agree over the extent to which it should pursue negotiations with the Americans. The War Minister, General Tojo Hideki, was pessimistic about the outcome of negotiations and was adamant that Japan had to go to war before the end of the year, when tropical monsoons would make operations difficult. Konoye wanted to negotiate for as long as possible. All agreed, however, that Japan could not withdraw from China.

These tensions partly explain the different diplomatic signals emanating from Tokyo during the following months. But the American and British governments were reluctant to take the Japanese overtures at face value. In an amazing feat of ingenuity and persistence US naval cryptanalysts had broken the Japanese diplomatic ciphers and the resulting intelligence, known as Magic, gave the Americans clear insight into Japanese intentions. Japan's decision on July 2 to strike south was known within a few days in Washington, London, and Canberra.

President Roosevelt also learned from Magic that the Japanese planned to continue diplomatic efforts while they secretly prepared for a military offensive. He was therefore well prepared when on July 24 the Japanese moved into southern Indochina. Two days later the USA, in agreement with the British and the Dutch, froze Japanese assets and applied a further embargo that reduced trade with Japan by three-quarters. That same day General Douglas MacArthur, a retired American officer commanding the Philippines Army, was recalled to the colors and appointed commander of the US army in the Far East. On August 1, Roosevelt ordered an embargo on high-octane gasoline and crude oil exports.

These embargoes had a devastating effect on the Japanese economy. In June 1941 a joint army–navy investigating committee concluded that Japan would run out of oil in mid-1944. Neither the Japanese government nor the Japanese people were willing to accept the massive loss of face that would have resulted from withdrawing from Indochina and ultimately from China. There was no alternative but to seize the resources they needed from Malaya and the Dutch East Indies. The Japanese navy's planners also knew that the USA would not remain neutral, and that with its forces in the Philippines the USA would strike at the flanks of the Japanese invasion fleets.

The Japanese armed forces had been preparing for war with the USA from the beginning of the year. The Commander-in-Chief of the Japanese Fleet, Admiral Yamamoto Isoruku, had served in the USA for several years and knew the power of the American industrial base. He was opposed to war, but became convinced that Japan's only hope was to destroy the US Pacific Fleet with a daring pre-emptive strike at its base at Pearl Harbor, Hawaii. The plan was approved and the Japanese navy secretly began training its pilots to undertake low-level torpedo attacks against ships in a remote bay similar to that at Pearl Harbor. Yamamoto finally selected the date for the attack – the morning of Sunday December 7 – when most of the US fleet, including its aircraft carriers, were usually in port for the weekend.

On September 6 the Japanese Cabinet met with Emperor Hirohito and decided to continue negotiations, while preparing to go to war if the negotiations were not successful by October 10. When October 10 passed without progress in the negotiations, the War Minister, Tojo, indicated that he had lost confidence in Konoye, who then resigned. On October 17 Tojo became Prime Minister, while retaining his post as War Minister. Tojo was determined to establish Japanese primacy in the Far East, to defeat the Western nations that had colonies in the Far East, to incorporate China into Japan, and to establish the East Asia Co-prosperity Sphere in the countries of southeast Asia.

On November 2 Tojo appeared before the Emperor and argued that Japan had to seize the moment. Three days later the Japanese government issued war orders and gave its diplomats until November 25 to solve the problem. On November 7 the USA deciphered Japanese diplomatic messages that showed that November 25 was a key date. Meanwhile, Japan offered not to seize any of the oil-producing islands if the USA agreed not to

interfere in China. Aware that Japan had already set a course for war, on November 26 the US Secretary of State, Cordell Hull, restated the USA's conditions – that Japan withdraw from both Indochina and China, accept the legitimacy of Chiang Kai-shek's government, and, in effect, withdraw from the Tripartite Pact with Germany and Italy.

Already Japanese forces were on the move. On November 17 the ships that were to attack Pearl Harbor left their ports and began gathering at an anchorage in the remote northern Kurile Islands. On November 26 Yamamoto sent Vice-Admiral Nagumo Chuichi, commander of the carrier strike force, a coded message: "Climb Mount Niitaka." It was the order to set sail for war. Nagumo's force included six of Japan's best aircraft carriers, two battleships, two cruisers, a destroyer screen, and eight support ships. Once they left the Kuriles they were to apply strict radio silence and to sail through the far northern Pacific Ocean, well away from shipping lanes.

The Allies had no knowledge of the carrier force's progress, but the Japanese could not keep their other war preparations secret. On November 26 Roosevelt was given intelligence that a large Japanese convoy carrying 50,000 troops was at sea south of Formosa. Next day Admiral Harold Stark, chief of US naval operations, sent a "war warning" to Admirals Husband Kimmel and Thomas Hart of the Pacific and Asiatic fleets at Pearl Harbor and Manila. The message said that negotiations with Japan had ceased and that an "aggressive move" by Japan was "expected within the next few days." Indications were that the Japanese might launch amphibious attacks against the Philippines, Thailand, Malaya, or possibly Borneo.

Although the Japanese intended to strike without warning, they still played out the diplomatic charade of presenting the USA with an ultimatum to rectify a list of grievances. This diplomatic note was to be presented to the US Secretary of State at 1:00 pm on Sunday, December 7. As soon as the 14-part message was transmitted from Tokyo to Japan's Washington Embassy, it was deciphered by the Americans and on Sunday morning it was passed to Roosevelt, who remarked, "This means war." The Japanese Embassy failed to decipher and translate the cable as quickly as the Americans, and the Japanese diplomats were not able to present the note formally to Cordell Hull until 2:30 pm. By then both Roosevelt and Hull knew that Hawaii had been under air attack for more than an hour. Japanese surprise had been complete.

The attack on Pearl Harbor

Before dawn on December 7 the Japanese fleet was 275 miles (440 km) north of Hawaii, while five midget submarines were already approaching Pearl Harbor. At 6:00 am the Japanese aircraft began to take off from the pitching decks of the aircraft carriers, and led by the veteran aviator Commander Fuchida Mitsuo, 183 planes gathered in formation: 49 Val bombers carrying armor-piercing bombs, 40 Kates with the deadly Long Lance torpedoes, and 43 Zero fighters to provide protection and to attack surface targets. As the Japanese aircraft made their way through the hills of northern Oahu, the air base and port lay unprepared on a sleepy Sunday morning. At anchor was almost the entire US Pacific Fleet. All that was missing were the two carriers, at sea with their escorts, including most of the heavy cruisers. At about 7:55 am the Japanese dive-bombers struck, followed 45 minutes later by a further 176 aircraft.

For the loss of 29 aircraft the Japanese sunk six battleships and damaged two. Three destroyers, three light cruisers, and four other vessels were also sunk or damaged. On

At 6:00 am on December 7, Japanese planes began to take off from six carriers sailing about 275 miles (440 km) north of Hawaii. (US National Archives)

The battleship *Arizona* in its anchorage in Pearl Harbor after the Japanese attack on December 7, 1941. An explosion in the forward magazine killed 1,103 crewmen, most being trapped below decks. The destruction of the American battleships forced the US navy to rely on its carriers. (US National Archives)

the airfields 164 aircraft were destroyed and another 128 damaged. Altogether, 2,403 servicemen and civilians were killed.

It was a tactical victory, but not the strategic victory for which the Japanese had hoped. In due course, all but three ships were repaired and returned to service. And the Japanese failed to destroy the US navy's extensive oil storage facilities, with a reserve of 4.5 million barrels. Had the oil and other essential dockyard facilities been destroyed, the US navy would have been forced to retreat to the West Coast. Further, while eight battleships had been put out of action, the carriers and heavy cruisers had escaped damage. Vice-Admiral Nagumo might well have ordered another attack later in the day. But he went for safety first and headed for home, loath to remain near to Hawaii, where

he might come under attack from the American carriers. The chance to inflict a crushing blow was lost.

Although the Japanese attack failed to cripple the US Pacific Fleet, it was a tremendous blow to American military pride. Admiral Kimmel was struck on the chest by a spent bullet while watching the attack from his office. "It would have been merciful had it killed me," he admitted to a fellow officer. Kimmel and Lieutenant-General Walter Short, commanding the US army on Hawaii, were relieved of their commands. Over the next four years there were seven investigations to discover why the Americans had been caught by surprise.

After the war a joint Congress investigation revealed that the USA had broken some of the Japanese codes and that information was available that might have indicated that the Japanese were going to attack Pearl Harbor. Blame was not apportioned to any individuals, but Kimmel and Short believed that they had been made scapegoats for the errors of others.

On December 8, 1941 the US President, Franklin Roosevelt, asked Congress to declare war. His opening words were memorable: "Yesterday, December 7, 1941 – a date which will live in infamy – the United States of America was suddenly and deliberately attacked." The surprise attack thus ensured that the USA would not rest until it had crushed Japan. (US National Archives)

In the ensuing years, some historians suggested that Roosevelt either deliberately provoked the Japanese or at least knew that they were going to attack Pearl Harbor, and did nothing, thereby ensuring that the USA entered the war without firing the first shot. Historians have not generally accepted this view. One of the most perceptive analysts, Roberta Wohlstetter, wrote in 1962: "We failed to anticipate Pearl Harbor not for want of the relevant materials but because of a plethora of irrelevant ones."

The conspiracy theory would not die, fueled by further revelations about the success of the Allied code-breakers. But Rear-Admiral Edwin Layton, chief intelligence officer at Pearl Harbor throughout the war, argued in 1985 that the intelligence débâcle was caused by intra- and inter-service squabbles in Washington. By the evening of December 6 the leaders in Washington knew that Japan would launch into war in a matter of hours rather than days, but there was no evidence that anyone suspected that Pearl Harbor would be a target.

Several authors have claimed that British intelligence broke the Japanese fleet code, used by Yamamoto to signal instructions to Nagumo, and that the British Prime Minister, Winston Churchill, failed to pass the information on to Roosevelt, ensuring that the USA entered the war and thus saving Britain from defeat. There is no evidence to prove this theory.

Malaya and the Philippines

While the Pearl Harbor attack was a tremendous surprise, elsewhere there was clear warning of Japanese intentions, even though the exact destination of their invasion convoys could not be determined. Soon after midnight on December 7–8, but because of the time difference several hours before the attack on Pearl Harbor, a Japanese invasion fleet began bombarding Kota Bharu in northern Malaya. During the morning, troops began landing there and at other locations along the Thai and Malayan coast.

The Japanese knew that they would have to deal with the 35 US B-17 bombers at Clark Field in the Philippines, but fog on Formosa prevented their aircraft from taking off before dawn to attack Clark. General MacArthur had been advised of the attack on Pearl Harbor, but failed to act decisively. When the main Japanese attack force reached Clark soon after midday, it caught most of the American aircraft on the ground. In a disaster to rival that at Pearl Harbor, the Americans lost half of their B-17 fleet and 86 other aircraft.

In less than 14 hours the Japanese had attacked Malaya, Hawaii, Thailand, the Philippines, Guam Island, Hong Kong, and Wake Island, in that order. The speculations of diplomats and military staffs about Japanese intentions had ended.

The course of the Pacific war

Between December 1941 and March 1942 Japanese forces conducted one of history's most successful series of military campaigns. Perhaps the most remarkable campaign took place in Malaya. It began on December 8 with the landing in northeast Malaya of troops from the Japanese Twenty-Fifth Army, under Lieutenant-General Yamashita Tomoyuki. Yamashita's force of 60,000 men was opposed by 88,000 British, Australian, Indian, and Malayan troops under Lieutenant-General Arthur Percival, but the Japanese naval and land-based aircraft completely outnumbered and outclassed the British air force. On December 10 the British suffered a devastating blow when Japanese aircraft sank the battleship *Prince of Wales* and the battle cruiser *Repulse* in the South China Sea.

Advancing more than 600 miles (1,000 km), by January 31, 1942 the Japanese had driven the Commonwealth forces back to Singapore. Although they had suffered heavily, the Commonwealth forces had, however, been reinforced and now numbered 85,000. Yamashita attacked with 35,000 troops, crossing the Johore Strait on the night of February 7/8. On February 15 Percival surrendered his force. Described by Winston Churchill as the "worst disaster in British military history," the fall of Singapore shattered British prestige in the Far East.

Elsewhere, the Japanese were conducting similar campaigns. During the second week of December they landed in the Philippines, with the main landing on December 22, 1941,

General Percival (right), accompanied by a Japanese officer, makes his way to meet General Yamashita to surrender his forces at Singapore on February 15, 1942. More than 130,000 Commonwealth troops became prisoners of war during the campaign. Yamashita's casualties numbered about 5,000. (Imperial War Museum, London, print from MARS, Lincs)

The conquest of Malaya, December 1941–February 1942

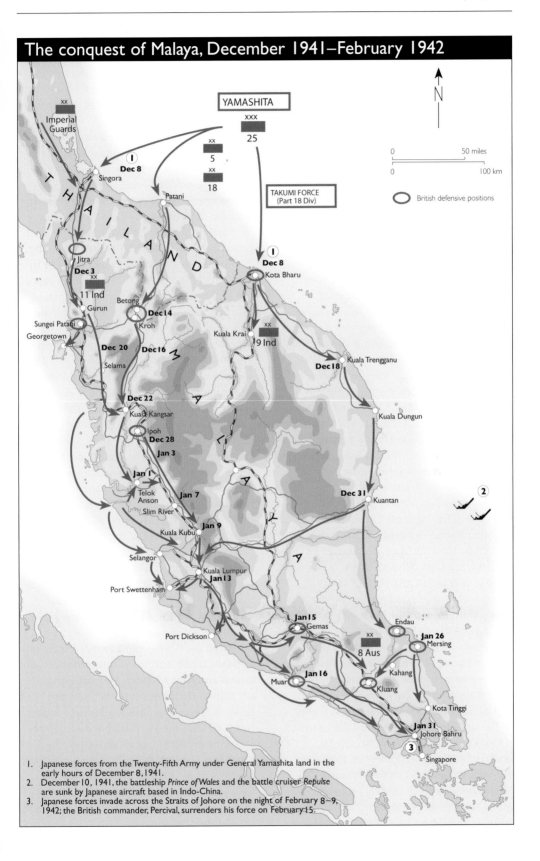

1. Japanese forces from the Twenty-Fifth Army under General Yamashita land in the early hours of December 8, 1941.
2. December 10, 1941, the battleship *Prince of Wales* and the battle cruiser *Repulse* are sunk by Japanese aircraft based in Indo-China.
3. Japanese forces invade across the Straits of Johore on the night of February 8–9, 1942; the British commander, Percival, surrenders his force on February 15.

by Lieutenant-General Homma Masaharu's Fourteenth Army, at Lingayen Gulf on Luzon. Realizing that his American and Filipino troops were no match for the Japanese, General MacArthur declared Manila an open city and withdrew into the Bataan peninsula, with his headquarters on Corregidor Island in Manila Bay. The Japanese occupied Manila on January 2, 1942. The troops on the Bataan peninsula resisted stoutly but were short of food and ammunition. On orders from President Roosevelt, on March 12 MacArthur left Corregidor by PT boat and, after transferring to an aircraft at Mindanao, continued to Australia. The force on Bataan surrendered on April 9, and MacArthur's successor, Lieutenant-General Jonathan Wainwright, surrendered on Corregidor on May 6.

The Japanese attacked Hong Kong on December 8, 1941. The garrison of 4,400 troops, including 800 Canadians, continued the resistance until Christmas Day. Also on December 8, Japanese planes bombed the US Pacific base at Wake Island. Shore batteries and US Marine fighter aircraft drove off an invasion force, but on December 23 a larger Japanese force overwhelmed the defenders.

With victory in sight in Malaya and the Philippines, the Japanese turned their attention to the Netherlands East Indies. To coordinate their defenses, on January 15, 1942 the Allies established ABDA (American–British–Dutch–Australian) Command with its headquarters on Java. Its commander, General Sir Archibald Wavell, was responsible for the defense of the area from Burma, through Singapore, to the East Indies and northern Australia, but his forces were not large enough and Allied coordination was poor.

Japanese forces seized Tarakan, off Borneo, on January 11, crushed the Australian garrison at Rabaul in New Britain on January 23, landed at Balikpapan, Borneo, on the same day, and reached the Celebes on January 24. The Japanese struck at Ambon on January 31, and in three days captured the Dutch and Australian garrison. On February 14 Japanese

paratroops landed on Sumatra, where they were joined by seaborne troops. Japanese air attacks on the Australian port of Darwin on February 19 provided protection for their invasion of West (Dutch) and East (Portuguese) Timor the following day.

On February 27 in the Java Sea, five American, British, Dutch, and Australian cruisers with nine destroyers, all under Dutch Rear-Admiral Karel Doorman, tried unsuccessfully to intercept the Japanese invasion fleet bound for Java. In the first fleet action of the Pacific War, the Allies lost two cruisers and three destroyers, and Doorman was killed. Next night the surviving cruisers, the Australian *Perth* and the USS *Houston*, engaged another Japanese invasion fleet in the Sunda Strait. They sank two ships before they too were sunk. The way was now clear for the Japanese invasion. The ABDA forces in Java formally surrendered on March 12, although Wavell and other senior officers had been evacuated earlier. It was the end of ABDA Command.

The Japanese landed in southern Thailand on December 8 to facilitate their Malayan campaign. Next day, the Thai Prime Minister ordered his forces to cease resistance and Thailand declared war on Britain and the USA the following month. In mid-January the Japanese Fifteenth Army in Thailand crossed into Burma. The British had two divisions (one Burmese and the other Indian), but they could not prevent the Japanese taking Rangoon on March 7. Fearful that the Burma Road – its supply lifeline – was being cut, China sent forces into Burma, but the Japanese were superior. They separated the Chinese and British forces, and by May 20 had driven the British out of Burma and back to India. Meanwhile, to strengthen their hold over their western flank, Admiral Nagumo's carrier fleet, which had attacked both Pearl Harbor and Darwin, entered the Indian Ocean and struck the British base at Colombo. Two British cruisers and several other ships, including a carrier, were sunk between April 5 and 9.

Japan's rapid success caught their planners unprepared. On January 5, 1942, when it looked as they though would achieve all their targets by the middle of March, the Chief of Staff of the Japanese Combined Fleet wrote in his diary: "Where shall we go from there? Shall we advance into Australia, attack Hawaii; or shall we prepare for the possibility of a Soviet sortie and knock them out if an opportunity arises?" For two months Imperial General Headquarters debated these questions.

The Japanese army resisted the navy's plan to invade Australia, as it could not spare the necessary 10 or perhaps 12 divisions from China or Manchuria. If the Red Army collapsed before the German blitzkrieg, Japan might launch an invasion of Siberia. Even more crucially, a major assault on Australia would require 1.5–2 million tons of shipping; most of this shipping was required to transport the newly won raw materials from southeast Asia to Japan. Instead, the army preferred an offensive in Burma and India.

Admiral Chester Nimitz (left), Commander-in-Chief of the US Pacific Fleet and the Pacific Ocean Area. After Pearl Harbor, Roosevelt told Nimitz to "get the. . .out to Hawaii and don't come back until the war is won." Easygoing and affable, he could be tough when necessary, was willing to take risks, and was an outstanding strategist. (US National Archives)

The navy was not unanimous about the need to invade Australia. Admiral Yamamoto wanted to attack Midway, in the central Pacific, to draw the US Pacific Fleet into battle. A compromise was reached: the invasions of Australia and India were put aside and on March 15 it was agreed to capture Port Moresby and the southern Solomons, and "to isolate Australia" by seizing Fiji, Samoa, and New Caledonia. The Japanese planned to form a defensive ring around their Greater East Asia Co-prosperity Sphere; if Australia could be isolated, it would no longer be a base for an American counteroffensive.

Coral Sea and Midway

In the midst of the Japanese offensive, the Allies struggled to reshape their Pacific strategy. Global strategy was to be determined by the Combined Chiefs of Staff, consisting of the American and British Chiefs of Staff. Priority was given to the war with Germany. The Pacific War was left in the hands of the US Joint Chiefs of Staff. The key figure was the newly appointed Commander-in-Chief of the US navy, Admiral Ernest King, who, despite the focus on Germany,

FOLLOWING PAGES Map
1. December 7, 1941, Japanese carrier-borne aircraft attack Pearl Harbor
2. December 8, 1941, Japan invades Malaya; February 15, 1942, Singapore surrenders
3. December 8–25, 1941, invasion of Hong Kong
4. December 10, 1941, Japanese invade Philippines; surrendered May 6, 1942
5. December 24, 1941, Wake Island captured by Japanese
6. January 11, 1942–March 8, 1942, invasion of Dutch East Indies
7. January 19–May 15, 1942, invasion of Burma
8. January 23–August 6, 1942, invasion of New Britain, Solomons, New Guinea, and part of Papua
9. February 19, 1942, Japanese carrier-borne and land-based aircraft attack Darwin
10. April 5, 1942, Japanese carrier-borne aircraft attack Colombo
11. May 4–8, 1942, Battle of the Coral Sea
12. May 31–June 1, 1942, Japanese submarines attack Sydney Harbor
13. June 3–6, 1942, Battle of Midway
14. June 6–7, 1942, Japanese land in Aleutian Islands

Japan's conquests December 1941–August 1942

Controlled by Japan, December 7, 1941

- - - - Controlled by Japan, August 6, 1942

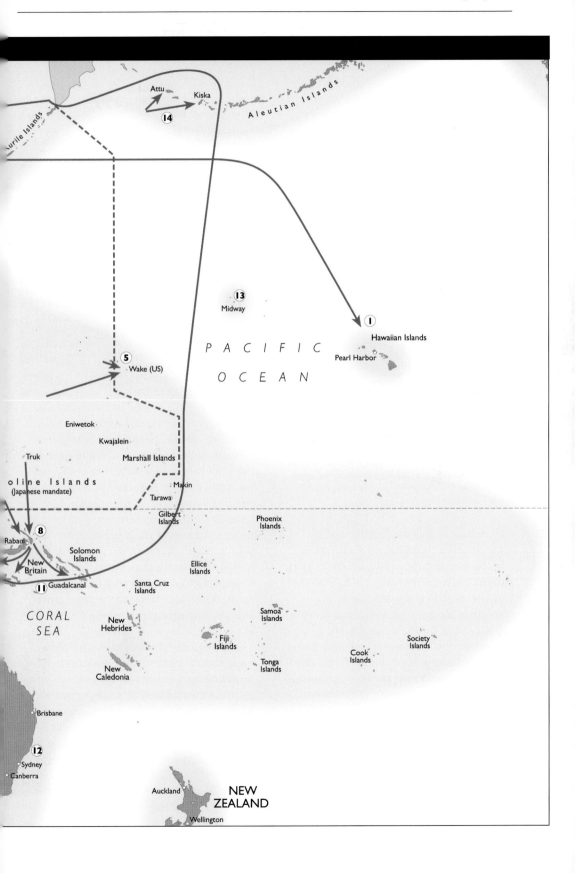

The crew of the carrier USS *Lexington* abandon ship while a destroyer maneuvers alongside, during the Battle of the Coral Sea, May 8, 1942. Leaking fuel fumes set off an uncontrollable fire and explosions. After she was abandoned, American destroyers finished her off. Only 216 of her total complement of 2,951 were lost. (US Navy/MARS, Lincs)

was anxious to revitalize Pacific strategy. Admiral Nimitz, with his headquarters at Pearl Harbor, had only three aircraft carriers, but was determined to take the fight to the Japanese as early as possible. General MacArthur became Commander-in-Chief of the Southwest Pacific Area, with his headquarters in Melbourne, Australia. His was an Allied command and included all of Australia's combat forces as well as relatively small numbers of American ships, planes, and combat troops.

Nimitz moved quickly and during February and March planes from his carriers raided Japanese bases in the Gilbert and Marshall Islands and Japanese shipping near New Guinea. On April 18, 16 B-25 bombers from the USS *Hornet*, under Colonel James Doolittle, raided Japan. The raid did little

damage, but Admiral Yamamoto now won his argument that he should strike at Midway.

Meanwhile, a Japanese invasion force set sail from Rabaul to seize Port Moresby, on the south coast of New Guinea. Warned by signals intelligence, Allied naval forces, including the carriers *Lexington* and *Yorktown*, rushed to intercept the Japanese in the Coral Sea. On May 7 and 8, in the first naval battle in which opposing ships never sighted each other, American aircraft sank the small carrier *Shoho* and damaged the large carrier *Shokaku*. The Americans lost the *Lexington*, while the *Yorktown* was damaged.

Although the Japanese had achieved a slight tactical victory, they called off their sea-borne invasion of Port Moresby, awaiting the conclusion of their attack on Midway in early June. Equally important, Japanese losses meant that Yamamoto's forces would be reduced for the Midway battle. The absence of one fleet carrier was perhaps critical to the outcome of that battle. The Battle of the Coral Sea gave the Allies vital breathing space in which to build up the force in New Guinea. It was the

American dive-bombers moving in to attack Japanese carriers during the Battle of Midway on June 4, 1942. American torpedo bombers had carried out futile attacks, losing 35 of 41 aircraft in the first attack. This exposed the Japanese fleet to US dive-bombers that soon reduced three carriers to burning wrecks. (US National Archives)

end of an unbroken run of successful Japanese invasions.

The Battle of Midway was the crucial battle of the Pacific War. When American code-breakers discovered that Admiral Nagumo's strike force of four carriers intended to attack Midway, Nimitz deployed his limited forces. *Yorktown* limped back to Pearl Harbor, was quickly repaired in an outstanding feat of engineering, and joined the American carrier task force of *Enterprise* and *Hornet*, under the careful, clear-thinking Rear-Admiral Raymond Spruance. Not expecting to encounter American carriers, on June 4 the Japanese were caught off-guard. By the end of the battle on June 7, the Japanese had lost all four fleet carriers, while *Yorktown* was damaged and finally sunk by a Japanese submarine. It was the first decisive defeat inflicted on the Japanese and changed the naval balance in the Pacific.

Japan now postponed its plans to seize New Caledonia, Fiji, and Samoa; instead, the capture of Port Moresby became even more urgent. With the loss of the carriers, an amphibious operation was no longer possible, and on June 7 Lieutenant-General Hyakutake Harukichi in Rabaul was ordered to plan a land approach over the forbidding Owen Stanley Ranges to Port Moresby. Strategically, the tide of war was beginning to turn, but the Japanese were still capable of mounting a deadly offensive.

Guadalcanal and New Guinea

The US navy's success at Midway encouraged the US Joint Chiefs of Staff in Washington, and on July 2, 1942 they ordered an offensive in the New Guinea–Solomon Islands area to recapture Rabaul. Because of jealousy between the US navy and the US army, the offensive was to be shared. In June the Americans had received reports that the Japanese were building an airstrip on Guadalcanal in the southern Solomon Islands. US naval forces under Vice-Admiral Robert Ghormley were ordered to seize several islands in the southern Solomons,

US Marines on the march to Matanikau, west of Henderson Field on Guadalcanal. The Matanikau battle began toward the end of September and the position was not secured until late October 1942, following a fierce Japanese counterattack. (AKG Berlin)

including Guadalcanal, for which he was allocated the 1st US Marine Division. Once the Marines had landed on Guadalcanal, MacArthur planned to occupy the Buna area on the north coast of Papua, where airstrips would be prepared to support his advance toward Rabaul.

Unfortunately for these plans, the Japanese moved first. Their advance troops landed at Buna on the night of July 21, to be met by only light resistance. The Japanese South Seas Detachment was now ordered to attack Port Moresby over the mountains. Belatedly, MacArthur began to send reinforcements to New Guinea.

The Japanese were thrown off-balance by the landing of the US Marines at Guadalcanal on August 7. Not pleased to be pushed off their new airstrip, the Japanese attacked the Americans with aircraft based at Rabaul. Vice-Admiral Jack Fletcher therefore withdrew his three carriers, exposing the remaining forces to the Japanese ships. On the night of August 8/9, in the Battle of Savo Island, Japanese cruisers sank the Australian cruiser

Canberra and three American cruisers. Following up this victory, the Japanese landed 1,000 men on Guadalcanal, but on August 21 they lost heavily in an attack on the perimeter of Henderson airfield. While the Americans held the airstrip they controlled the surrounding seas by day; but at night the Japanese dominated, bringing in more reinforcements in an attempt to seize the vital airstrip.

In Papua, MacArthur's Australian forces faced a similar challenge. The Japanese offensive began on August 26 with two simultaneous attacks – one on the Kokoda Trail that wound over the Owen Stanley Ranges, and the other a landing by Japanese Marines at Milne Bay on the southeast tip of New Guinea. Fearful for his own position, MacArthur tried to blame the Australians for their allegedly poor fighting ability. But by September 6 two Australian brigades at Milne Bay had defeated the Japanese, forcing them to evacuate. On the Kokoda Trail, however, Australian troops conducted a desperate withdrawal. Eventually the Japanese failed;

the track was much more difficult than expected and they had made insufficient provision for supplies. Importantly, the Guadalcanal campaign caused the Japanese high command in Rabaul to divert resources to that area, and eventually to order a halt to the Owen Stanley offensive.

The fighting on and around Guadalcanal turned into a campaign of attrition. During September and October the Japanese made repeated efforts to recover Henderson airfield. In the Battle of Bloody Ridge 2,000 Japanese attacked in massed waves, and some came within 3,000 ft (900 m) of the airfield. If they had taken it, they might well have won the campaign. Lieutenant-Colonel Merrit A. Edson, commanding the force defending the ridge, was awarded the Congressional Medal of Honor. The

Australian soldiers of the 39th Battalion on the Kokoda Trail in August 1942. Short of supplies, the Australians conducted a fighting withdrawal in the Owen Stanley Ranges that bought time for reinforcements to arrive and caused the Japanese to exhaust their supplies. (Australian War Memorial)

defenders were supported by Marine aircraft of the "Cactus Air Force" operating from the airfield, but in October Japanese ships bombarded the airfield, putting it temporarily out of action. As reinforcements arrived, the Marines gradually widened their perimeter, meeting strong resistance from the Japanese on the surrounding hills and in the jungle-filled valleys.

Naval battles continued around Guadalcanal, and Fletcher was relieved of his command. One American carrier was sunk and another damaged. On October 18 Vice-Admiral William Halsey relieved Ghormley of command of the campaign. In the Battle of Santa Cruz, the carrier *Hornet* was lost and *Enterprise* was damaged. The naval battle of Guadalcanal began on November 12 and lasted for three days; in

Admiral William (Bull) Halsey assumed command of the Guadalcanal campaign in October 1942 and remained in command of the Solomons campaign until March 1944. He and Admiral Spruance then alternated as commander of the Pacific Fleet's main operational force, known as the Third Fleet when under his command, and the Fifth Fleet when under Spruance. (US National Archives)

the first 24 minutes the Americans lost six ships and the Japanese three, including a battleship. Eventually the odds began to tilt toward the Americans.

In New Guinea the 7th Australian Division advanced back over the Kokoda Trail to the north coast, where it was joined by the US 32nd Division. Exhausted, sick, and with little support, the Australians and Americans were confronted by well-constructed Japanese defenses in jungle and swamp. MacArthur unreasonably demanded a swift victory, telling the American corps commander, Lieutenant-General Robert Eichelberger, "to take Buna, or not come back alive." By the time the Japanese had been driven into the sea at Sanananda on January 22, 1943, they had suffered more than 13,000 killed. The Australians lost more than 2,000 killed and the Americans more than 600. Almost 20,000 Australian and American troops were sick from malaria.

The Japanese faced a similar outcome on Guadalcanal, but in one of the crucial decisions of the Pacific War their high command decided to move to the strategic defensive and ordered an evacuation. This took place in February. During the campaign the Japanese lost perhaps 24,000 killed, while American fatal casualties numbered some 1,600. The Japanese had lost many of their best trained pilots and their naval air force never recovered from these losses.

The campaigns in New Guinea and Guadalcanal were fought in thick, tropical jungles and fetid swamps. Resupply was difficult, and in New Guinea the Allies relied on native porters and airdrops. Tropical illnesses were as deadly as the enemy's bullets.

The Japanese made one last offensive thrust, toward Wau in New Guinea, but this was thwarted when an Australian brigade was flown into the area. Seeking to build up their defenses, the Japanese created the Eighteenth Army and planned to reinforce New Guinea. Warned by signals intelligence and reconnaissance aircraft, the commander of the Allied air force in the Southwest Pacific Area, the highly capable Lieutenant-General

Japanese shipping under attack by American and Australian aircraft during the Battle of the Bismarck Sea, fought between March 2 and 4, 1943. The Japanese lost eight transports and four destroyers; of almost 7,000 troops on the transports, about half perished. (Australian War Memorial)

George Kenney, ordered the convoy to be intercepted in the Bismarck Sea.

Allied code-breakers also gave warning that Admiral Yamamoto would be visiting Bougainville in the northern Solomons. American P-38 Lightnings from Henderson Field were directed to his destination and on April 13, 1943 they downed his aircraft in flames. It was a further blow to the Japanese, who were already on the defensive in the southwest Pacific. Yamamoto was succeeded by Admiral Koga Mineichi as Commander-in-Chief of the Combined Fleet.

Aleutian Islands campaign

On the night of June 6, 1942, the Japanese landed 1,200 troops on remote Attu Island, at the western end of the Aleutian Islands – an island chain that projected 1,000 nautical miles (1,150 miles; 1,1852 km) from Alaska into the northern Pacific Ocean. Next day a small force took Kiska, another westerly island. The islands were undefended and had few inhabitants. The Japanese operation was partly to prevent the Americans from using the islands as a base for an attack on northern Japan, but mainly a diversion for the Midway operation. The Japanese occupations posed little threat, but as the islands were American territory there was public agitation for their recovery.

In response, the US Eleventh Air Force mounted a protracted bombing campaign, while American warships tried to prevent the Japanese from reinforcing their garrisons. These were extremely difficult operations as the islands were often shrouded in fog and rain. In March 1943, in one of the Pacific War's few "fleet actions" in open seas, American and Japanese cruisers pounded each other, with the Americans lucky to survive. But the Japanese fleet turned back and the Japanese admiral was dismissed from his command.

On May 11, 1943 the US 7th Infantry Division landed on Attu, where it faced fierce opposition, culminating in a suicidal Japanese bayonet charge on May 29. The USA lost 600 killed; only 28 Japanese were captured and 2,351 bodies were counted.

In a daring operation, on the night of July 28/29, 1943, under cover of fog, the Japanese navy evacuated its garrison of more than 5,000 troops from Kiska. The 34,000 American and Canadian troops who landed there on August 15 took several days to discover that they faced no opposition. For the Japanese, the campaign had been a disastrous waste of men and matériel when they had been under increasing pressure in the south and southwest Pacific.

The advance toward Rabaul

In January 1943 Roosevelt and Churchill met with their senior military advisers at Casablanca, Morocco, to set the strategic direction for the coming year. Although the leaders relegated the Pacific War to fifth on the list of priorities (after the Atlantic, Russia, the Mediterranean, and the United Kingdom), the directive of July 2, 1942 to capture Rabaul remained unchanged. Again the tasks were shared. Forces from the South Pacific Area, under Admiral Halsey, would advance from Guadalcanal toward Rabaul with the intermediate objective of Bougainville in the northern Solomons. Meanwhile, MacArthur's forces would seize the Huon peninsula in New Guinea and the western end of New Britain. The total operation was known as Operation Cartwheel.

Opposing the Allied forces was Lieutenant-General Imamura Hitoshi's Eighth Area Army with its headquarters at Rabaul. Lieutenant-General Hyakutake's Seventeenth Army defended the Solomons and New Britain with three divisions, while Lieutenant-General Adachi Hatazo's Eighteenth Army, also with three divisions, was in New Guinea. The Japanese strength was between 80,000 and 90,000, but they could be reinforced by about 60,000 within three weeks. The Japanese had about

RIGHT Map
Land operations
1. August 7, 1942, Americans land at Guadalcanal; Japanese withdraw on February 7, 1943
2. August 25–September 6, 1942, Japanese landing at Milne Bay is defeated by Australians
3. August 26–November 2, 1942, Japanese advance over the Kokoda Trail to within 97 miles (60 km) of Port Moresby and are then driven back to Kokoda by the Australians
4. November 16, 1942–January 22, 1943, US and Australian troops defeat Japanese at Buna, Gona, and Sanananda
5. January 28–September 11, 1943, Japanese attack Wau and are driven back to Salamaua by the Australians
6. June 30, 1943, Americans land on New Georgia
7. June 30, 1943, Americans land at Nassau Bay
8. August 15, 1943, Americans land on Vella Lavella
9. September 4, 1943, Australians land at Lae
10. September 5, 1943, Australians land at Nadzab and later advance up Markham Valley
11. September 22, 1943, Australians land at Finschhafen
12. November 1, 1943, Americans land on Bougainville
13. December 15 and 26, 1943, Americans land on New Britain
14. February 15, 1944, New Zealanders land at Green Island
15. January 2, 1944, Americans land at Saidor
16. February 29, 1944, Americans land on Los Negros
17. March 20, 1944, Americans land at Emirau
18. April 22, 1944, Americans land at Hollandia and Aitape
19. April 24, 1944, Australians enter Madang

Naval battles
A Savo Island, August 9, 1942
       Cape Esperance, October 11, 1942
       Guadalcanal, November 12–15, 1942
       Tassafronga, November 30, 1942
B Eastern Solomons, August 24, 1942
C Santa Cruz Island, October 26, 1942
D Bismarck Sea, March 2–4, 1943
E Kula Gulf, July 5–6, 1943
F Kolombangara, July 12–13, 1943
G Vella Gulf, August 6–7, 1943
H Vella Lavella, October 6–7, 1943
I   Empress Augusta Bay, November 2, 1943

320 combat aircraft, while about 270 others could be flown in within 48 hours.

The Cartwheel operation began on June 30, 1943 when Halsey's troops made their main landings on New Georgia and Rendova. The New Georgia landing soon turned into a hard-grinding battle, with three American divisions deployed under Major-General Oswald Griswold. Meanwhile the Japanese dispatched reinforcements from Rabaul, escorted by warships that clashed

Allied operations in New Guinea and the Solomons, August 1942–April 1944

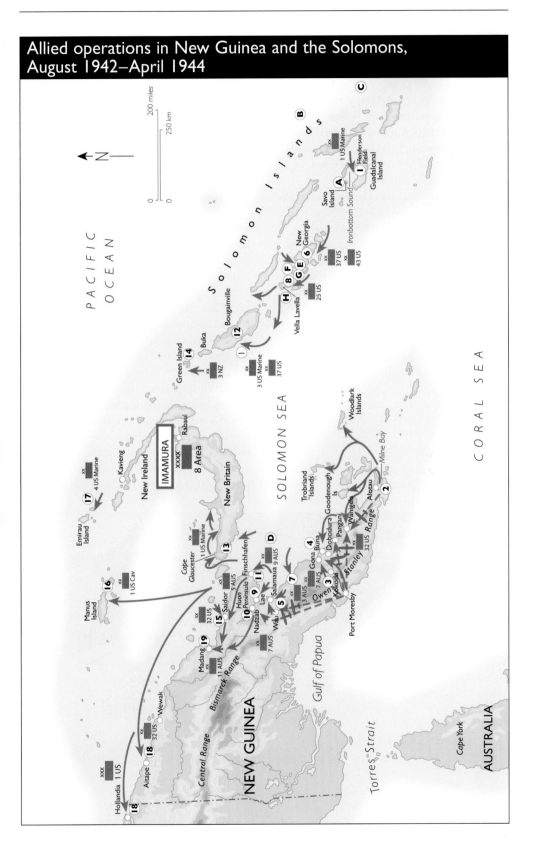

200 miles
250 km

N

PACIFIC OCEAN

Solomon Islands

C

B

Henderson Field
1 US Marine
Guadalcanal Island

A
Savo Island
Ironbottom Sound

New Georgia
37 US
43 US

F
E
8
G
H
25 US
Vella Lavella

Bougainville

12

Buka
Green Island
14
3 NZ
I
3 US Marine
37 US

Kavieng
17
4 US Marine
New Ireland

Emirau Island

Rabaul
IMAMURA
8 Area
New Britain

SOLOMON SEA

Trobriand Islands
Woodlark Islands

CORAL SEA

Cape Gloucester
1 US Marine
13

Manus Island
16
1 US Cav

D
Finschhafen
9 AUS
Huon Peninsula
11
Salamaua
5 AUS
7
Lae
Saidor
5
15
32 US
Nadzab
10
Wau
7 AUS

Goodenough Is
Dobodura
Buna
4
Gona
Pangani
3 AUS
Kokoda
3
7 AUS
32 US
Wanigela
Owen Stanley Range
Milne Bay
Alotau
2

Madang
19
11 AUS
Bismarck Range

Wewak
32 US
18

Aitape
Hollandia 1 US
18
1 US

Central Range

NEW GUINEA

Gulf of Papua

Port Moresby

Torres Strait

Cape York

AUSTRALIA

with the US navy. Superior in night fighting, the Japanese navy sank or damaged several American and Australian ships. But in one engagement three Japanese transports were sunk with the loss of perhaps 1,500 men drowned. By mid-September, when the Japanese withdrew from New Georgia, they had lost more than 2,000 killed; American deaths exceeded 1,000. American forces jumped to Vella Lavela, and by October, American and New Zealand troops had landed on several islands near to Bougainville.

On November 1 the 3rd US Marine Division landed at Empress Augusta Bay on the west coast of Bougainville, bypassing a large Japanese concentration at the south of the island. Next morning a US navy task force destroyed a cruiser and a destroyer from the Japanese Eighth Fleet. When a powerful Japanese task force under Vice-Admiral Kurita Takeo appeared at Rabaul, Halsey took a great risk and sent his two-carrier task force within

MacArthur's land forces were nominally under the Australian General Sir Thomas Blamey (right), but most American operations were controlled by the commander of the US Sixth Army, Lieutenant-General Walter Krueger (left). Tough and experienced, Blamey commanded New Guinea Force, which consisted of mainly Australian units. (Australian War Memorial)

range of Japanese air power. Supported by Kenney's land-based Fifth Air Force, US naval aircraft caused such damage that Kurita withdrew to Truk. Further Allied air attacks forced the Japanese to withdraw their air and naval units from Rabaul. In March 1944 the American forces resisted a full-scale Japanese counteroffensive on Bougainville. Thereafter there was a virtual truce until the Australians took over from the Americans toward the end of the year.

The fighting in the New Guinea area was marked by fewer naval engagements but larger land operations than in the Solomons. Between March and August 1943, the 3rd Australian Division slogged through jungle-covered hills from Wau toward Salamaua. The Japanese Fourth Air Army rushed additional planes to New Guinea, but, warned by Allied code-breakers, and by deploying aircraft to newly constructed forward airfields, Kenney's Fifth Air Force caught the Japanese planes on the ground at Wewak, with devastating losses.

On September 4 the 9th Australian Division conducted an amphibious landing near Lae, while in the following days the 7th Australian Division landed by air at Nadzab airstrip once it had been secured by

Troops of the 9th Australian Division landing at Finschhafen on the Huon peninsula on September 22, 1943. The Japanese counterattacked strongly and the Australians did not take their main bastion at Sattelberg until November 25. (Australian War Memorial)

American paratroops. Salamaua fell on September 11 and Lae on the 15th. After landing at Finschhafen, the Australians then continued along the New Guinea coast. Inland, the 7th Division cleared the Markham and Ramu valleys, where airfields were constructed for the Fifth Air Force, and pressed over the mountain range toward Madang. As in earlier campaigns, the climate, terrain, and vegetation provided an additional challenge.

American troops began landing on the southern coast of New Britain on December 15, with the main landing by the 1st US Marine Division at Cape Gloucester on December 26, where, after hard fighting, they established a perimeter. On January 2, 1944 the 32nd US Division landed at Saidor on the New Guinea coast. The Japanese 20th and 51st Divisions escaped, but they had been roundly defeated. Between March 1943 and April 1944 the Australians, under Blamey, deployed five infantry divisions, losing about 1,200 killed. Japanese losses numbered about 35,000.

The completion of the Cartwheel operation showed that the Americans and Australians had learned much about jungle warfare. In Malaya, Burma, the Philippines, and New Guinea the Japanese had caught their opponents off-guard. Lightly equipped and accustomed to hard living, the Japanese infantry moved quickly through deep jungle, bypassing static Allied positions. On the defensive, the Japanese constructed well-camouflaged strongpoints and fought with determination and skill. Their commanders perhaps lacked imagination in planning and did not seem to appreciate fully the effectiveness of massed firepower. As the Americans began to dominate the seas, the Japanese defenders (for whom surrender was not an option) often had little alternative but to fight to the death.

The Americans had to learn about jungle warfare in action and at first seemed bewildered by it. They learned quickly, but fought the war in their own way. As an American divisional historian put it: "The Yank style of fighting was to wait for the artillery and let the big guns blast the enemy positions as barren of all life as possible. It saved many American lives and got better results although it took longer." More broadly, the Americans brought to bear the full range of naval and air resources to support their land operations. All of this was backed by a massive logistic effort.

Although many of the Australian units had already fought in the Middle East, they still had to adapt to jungle conditions, and they concentrated especially on patrolling skills. They did not have the same weight of firepower and lavish supplies as the Americans, but were still superior to the Japanese in this regard. The Americans and Australians had far better medical support than the Japanese, especially for coping with tropical diseases such as malaria.

The island-hopping campaigns

Admiral King had always advocated using American naval power to attack the Japanese in the central Pacific, but MacArthur had argued for resources to enable him to advance through New Guinea toward the Philippines. If both approaches could be sustained, then they would throw the Japanese off-balance, but it was not until the latter months of 1943 that the US navy began to gather the strength necessary to prosecute a campaign in the central Pacific. At the time of Pearl Harbor, the US navy had only three carriers in the Pacific; by late 1943 Nimitz had 10 fast large and medium carriers, seven escort carriers, and a dozen battleships. These formed the key elements of the Fifth Fleet under Vice-Admiral Spruance.

Toward the end of 1943 this force began conducting raids on Japanese island bases, and on November 20, 1943 US Marine and army units landed on Tarawa and Makin atolls in the Gilbert Islands. Tarawa was a bitter fight, but Makin was taken relatively

On November 20, 1943, the 2nd Marine Division landed on the heavily defended Tarawa atoll in the Gilbert Islands. In a bitter and bloody five-day battle the Marines lost 1,000 killed and the Japanese their entire garrison of 5,000. (AKG Berlin)

easily. American attention now turned to the Marshall Islands with the US Navy's fast carrier task force raiding the islands in late December 1943 and early January 1944. On January 31, US Marine and army troops landed on Kwajalein Island. Eniwetok fell on February 17, six weeks ahead of schedule. Meanwhile, American carriers under Rear-Admiral Marc Mitscher heavily raided the Japanese naval base at Truk.

With the US navy moving faster than expected in the central Pacific, MacArthur

was fearful of being left behind and on February 29, 1944, in a daring "raid," his forces seized Los Negros in the Admiralty Islands. All ideas of attacking Rabaul were now abandoned; the huge Japanese garrison was to play little further part in the war. Instead, MacArthur directed a series of landings by American troops along the northern New Guinea coast that isolated 40,000 Japanese forces in the Wewak area. His forces took Aitape and Hollandia on April 23, Wakde on May 17, Biak on May 27, Noemfoor on July 2, and Sansapor on July 30. In three months he had advanced over 850 miles (1,400 km). With no carriers of his own, and receiving limited carrier support from the Central Pacific, MacArthur's forces constructed airfields at each landing to provide land-based air support for the next assault.

While MacArthur was advancing, Nimitz was focusing on the Mariana Islands. The key islands were Saipan, Guam, and Tinian, whose airfields were within bombing range of Japan. Realizing the danger, the Commander-in-Chief of the Japanese Combined Fleet (now Admiral Toyoda Soemu) ordered nine carriers and 450 aircraft to gather for a concerted attack on the Americans. Admiral Spruance commanded the invasion, to be covered by Mitscher's Task Force 58, now with 15 carriers and 1,000 planes. The invasion force included nearly 130,000 troops (only 22,500 fewer than in the opening phase of Operation Overlord at Normandy on June 6 – nine days earlier). The invasion force was carried in 535 ships.

Carrier strikes began on June 11, with troops of the 5th Amphibious Corps under Marine Lieutenant-General Holland (Howlin' Mad) Smith landing on Saipan on June 15. Japanese carrier- and land-based aircraft struck the US fleet on June 19, but were totally outclassed by the American aircraft and their more skillful pilots. In the "Great Marianas Turkey Shoot," the Japanese lost 400 aircraft, while the USA lost 30. Three Japanese carriers were sunk – two by American submarines. Onshore, the Marine and army troops had a savage battle against 32,000 defenders. The Japanese conducted suicide charges, while Japanese civilians leapt

to their death from high cliffs. It was July 9 before Saipan was secured. Total Japanese deaths numbered 30,000. Meanwhile, US Marine and army troops captured Guam and Tinian. The defeat of the Japanese carrier force and the seizure of the Marianas – Japanese mandated territory since World War I – were a severe blow to the Japanese high command. On July 18 Tojo resigned as Prime Minister and War Minister. Lieutenant-General Koiso Kuniaki succeeded him as Prime Minister.

Burma

While the operations in the southwest and central Pacific areas dominated the attention of the Americans, the Australians, and the Japanese navy during 1943 and 1944, Japanese army units were heavily engaged in Burma.

By May 1942 the Japanese army had driven the British into India and had pushed

General Sir William Slim was one of the outstanding commanders of the war. He commanded the Burma Corps during the 1942 retreat and the Fourteenth Army in the defensive battles of 1944 and the successful invasion of Burma in 1944–45. (National Army Museum)

several Chinese divisions back to the northern borders. In India the British–Indian Army began a painful process of expansion and retraining. Most of the units came from India with a large proportion of British officers, but eventually the forces that would retake Burma would include many nationalities – Indians, Burmese, Chinese, Gurkhas, troops from British East and West Africa, as well as British and Americans. As in the southwest Pacific, the campaigns were fought in jungle and in a trying climate, the seasonal monsoons making movement extremely difficult.

The first offensives began in the coastal Arakan area, between October 1942 and May 1943, but the Japanese drove back the British divisions in further morale-shattering defeats. The only success seemed to be that achieved by a brigade of special forces – the Chindits – under the eccentric Brigadier Orde Wingate, inserted into north-central Burma in February 1943. Actual success was slight, but the Chindits' exploits boosted morale.

In October 1943 the Allied Southeast Asia Command was formed under Admiral Lord Louis Mountbatten, with its headquarters in Ceylon. Mountbatten's tasks were to increase pressure on the Japanese and thus force them to transfer forces from the Pacific theater, to maintain the airborne supply route to China, and to open a land supply route through northern Burma. General Sir William Slim, commander of the Fourteenth Army, was to undertake three offensives into Burma: the 15th Corps (Lieutenant-General Philip Christison) would advance in the Arakan; the 4th Corps (Lieutenant-General Geoffrey Scoones) would prepare for an attack into central Burma from Imphal; and Northern Combat Area Command would thrust into northern Burma to open a route into China. This latter force, under the cantankerous American Lieutenant-General Joseph Stilwell, included two Chinese divisions and a brigade of Americans known as Merrill's Marauders; their advance would be supported by the Chindits, now numbering several brigades.

The commander of the Japanese Burma Area Army, Lieutenant-General Kawabe

Masakazu, decided to pre-empt this offensive by striking into India. If he gained a foothold for the Indian National Army – a force of Indian troops under Japanese control – he might even precipitate a revolt in India against British rule. The first Japanese offensive began as a diversion in Arakan in February 1944, where the British were also beginning an offensive. In bitter fighting around the "Admin Box," two Indian divisions defeated the attack and resumed their offensive.

The main Japanese offensive began in March 1944 when the Fifteenth Army with more than three divisions, under Lieutenant-General Mutuguchi Renya, crossed into India heading for Imphal and Kohima. The British 4th Corps was surrounded in the Imphal area and at Kohima. But as the Japanese had now been defeated in Arakan, Slim was able to fly in a division from there. Meanwhile, the defensive positions around Imphal were supplied by a huge effort by American and British transport aircraft. The 33rd Corps under Lieutenant-General Montague Stopford was deployed from India to relieve Kohima. Short of supplies and heavy weapons, the Japanese took dreadful casualties in an effort to break through into India. On May 31, they

FOLLOWING PAGES Map
1. August 7, 1942, US forces land at Guadalcanal
2. September 1942, Australians defeat Japanese at Milne Bay and advance back over Kokoda Trail
3. June 30, 1943, US forces land at New Georgia
4. June 30–December 1943, US and Australian forces land in New Guinea and New Britain
5. May–August 1943, US and Canadian forces recover Aleutian islands
6. November 20, 1943, US forces invade Tarawa and Makin islands
7. January 31–February 17, 1944, US forces land on Kwajalein and Eniwetok islands
8. March 15–June 22, 1944, Japanese invasion of north-eastern India defeated
9. April 22–July 30, 1944, US forces advance along New Guinea coast from Hollandia to Sansapor
10. April 1944, Japanese begin Ichigo offensive in China
11. June 15, 1944, US forces land at Saipan
12. July 21, 1944, US forces land at Guam
13. September 15, US forces land in Palau Islands and at Morotai

The Allied counteroffensive, August 1942–September 1944

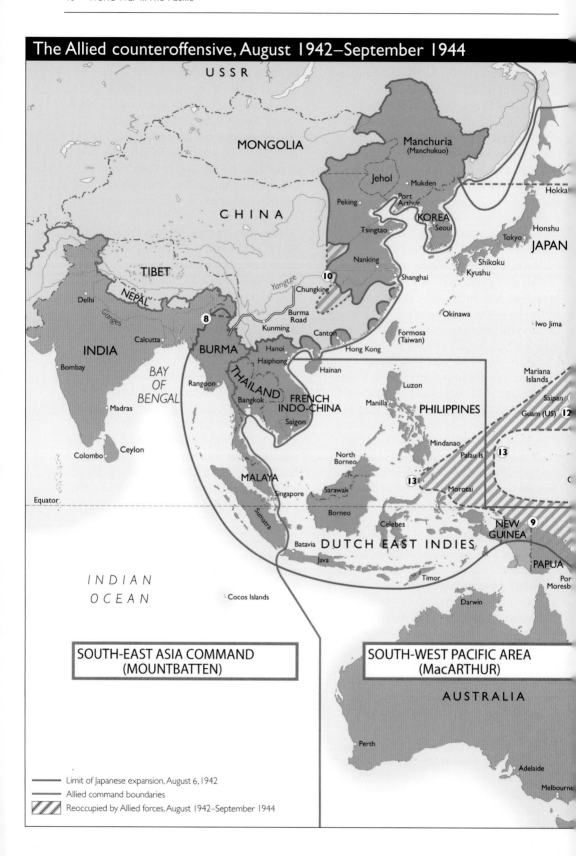

USSR

MONGOLIA

Manchuria
(Manchukuo)

Jehol · Mukden

Hokka

CHINA

Peking

Port
Arthur

KOREA

Honshu

Tsingtao

Seoul

Tokyo

JAPAN

Nanking

Shikoku

Kyushu

TIBET

Yangtze

Chungking

Shanghai

NEPAL

Delhi

Ganges

⑧

Burma
Road

Okinawa

Iwo Jima

⑩

Kunming

Canton

INDIA

Calcutta

BURMA

Hanoi

Hong Kong

Formosa
(Taiwan)

Bombay

Haiphong

THAILAND

Rangoon

BAY
OF
BENGAL

Hainan

Luzon

Mariana
Islands

Madras

Bangkok

FRENCH
INDO-CHINA

Manilla

PHILIPPINES

Saipan

Guam (US) ⑫

Saigon

Colombo

Ceylon

North
Borneo

Mindanao

Palau Is ⑬

MALAYA

Singapore

Sarawak

⑬

Morotai

⑬

Celebes

NEW
GUINEA ⑨

Equator

Borneo

Batavia   DUTCH EAST INDIES

PAPUA

Java

Timor

Por
Moresb

INDIAN
OCEAN

Cocos Islands

Darwin

SOUTH-EAST ASIA COMMAND
(MOUNTBATTEN)

SOUTH-WEST PACIFIC AREA
(MacARTHUR)

AUSTRALIA

Perth

Adelaide

Melbourne

——— Limit of Japanese expansion, August 6, 1942
——— Allied command boundaries
▧ Reoccupied by Allied forces, August 1942–September 1944

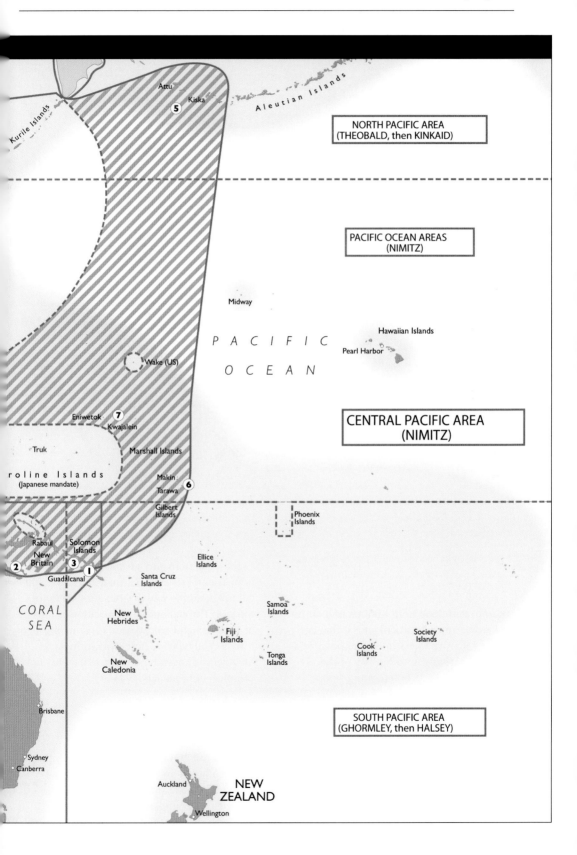

NORTH PACIFIC AREA
(THEOBALD, then KINKAID)

PACIFIC OCEAN AREAS
(NIMITZ)

CENTRAL PACIFIC AREA
(NIMITZ)

SOUTH PACIFIC AREA
(GHORMLEY, then HALSEY)

Attu

Kiska

⑤

Aleutian Islands

Kurile Islands

Midway

Hawaiian Islands

Pearl Harbor

P A C I F I C

O C E A N

Wake (US)

Eniwetok ⑦

Kwajalein

Truk

Marshall Islands

roline Islands
(Japanese mandate)

Makin

Tarawa ⑥

Gilbert
Islands

Phoenix
Islands

Rabaul   Solomon
Islands

New
Britain

② ③ ①

Guadalcanal

Santa Cruz
Islands

Ellice
Islands

CORAL
SEA

New
Hebrides

Fiji
Islands

Samoa
Islands

Society
Islands

Cook
Islands

Tonga
Islands

New
Caledonia

Brisbane

Sydney

Canberra

Auckland

NEW
ZEALAND

Wellington

British troops in carriers from the 33rd Corps advancing down the Imphal-Kohima road in June 1944. The 33rd Corps had relieved the besieged garrison at Kohima before opening the road to Imphal. The 4th Corps had fought a grim defensive battle at Imphal. (MARS)

began to withdraw from Kohima and on July 18 Kawabe and Mutugachi agreed that no further offensive operations were possible. It had been a disastrous offensive: of the invading force of 85,000 fighting troops, 53,000 became casualties, 30,000 being killed. The way was clear for Slim to advance into Burma, even though monsoonal rains made movement difficult.

Meanwhile, the Northern Combat Area Command had been advancing south, while the Chindits had been inserted across the Japanese lines of communication. Despite problems with Allied cooperation, on May 17 the Americans took Myitkyina airfield, from which supplies could be flown into China. The Japanese held the town until August 3. Several Chinese divisions also advanced into Burma from Yunan Province, but these offensives still did not open the way to China until later in the year. Throughout these operations a force of 17,000 engineers had been constructing a road and oil pipeline from Ledo in India to Myitkyina. The land route into China was not complete until January 1945.

China

The war in China was not a simple conflict between Japan and the Allies. The Allies accepted the Nationalist leader, Chiang Kai-shek, as commander-in-chief of the China theater, but the Chinese Communist

Party, under Mao Tse-tung, controlled much of northwest China and conducted extensive and successful guerrilla operations against the Japanese. Semi-autonomous warlords with their own armies ruled several provinces; nominally they were under direction from the Nationalist government at Chungking, but sometimes they cooperated with the Japanese in operations against the communists. In 1938 the Japanese had established a Chinese puppet government, under Wang Ching-wei, with its capital at Nanking. Wang's army of up to 900,000 conducted operations against both the communists and the warlords.

During 1941 and 1942 the Japanese conducted ruthless punishment operations in northern and central China, but by 1943 they were hard-pressed by the communist guerrilla campaign. The Japanese then pursued a pacification policy, hoping that eventually the Wang puppet government might assume control, or that it might conclude an agreement with the Nationalists.

Chiang Kai-shek realized that the Allies were going to win the war and he wanted to preserve his armies for a future war against the communists. But he needed to give the impression that he was fighting the Japanese in order to maintain the flow of American arms and equipment. "Vinegar Joe" Stilwell believed that with adequate training and equipment the Chinese armies could perform well. Influenced by Major-General Claire Chennault, who commanded the American Volunteer Group (the Flying Tigers), Chiang placed his faith in air power.

The American operations in northern Burma were dominated by the desire to open

The Chinese Generalissimo, Chiang Kai-shek, with his wife and his US Chief of Staff, Lieutenant-General "Vinegar Joe" Stilwell, at Maymo, Burma, in April 1942. Stilwell had a low regard for Chiang, whom he called "the peanut." Stilwell also commanded the American forces in Burma. (US National Archives)

The Allied invasion of Burma 1944–1945

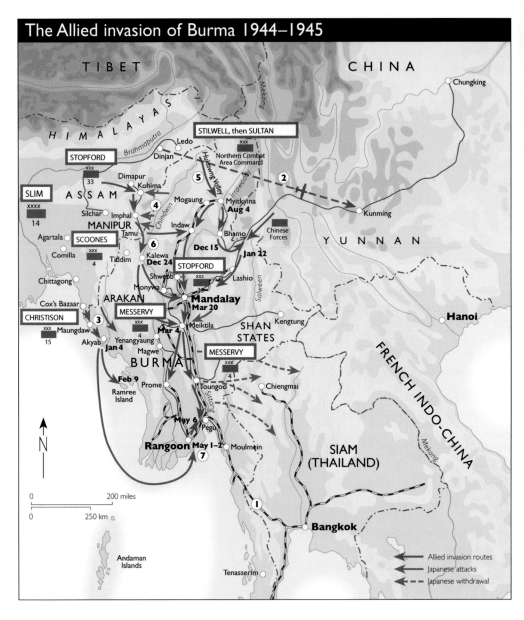

a route to China. This would enable them to build up the Nationalist armies as a viable force, and to use China as a base for air operations against Japanese ships in the South China Sea and even against Japan. Until a land route could be opened, the Nationalists and Chennault's small air force (never more than 200 aircraft) had to be supplied by air. American transport aircraft flew from makeshift airfields in India's northeastern Assam, 500 miles (800 km) over 13,000 ft (4,000 m) mountains to Kunming

in southern China. Flying "the hump" at high altitudes in turbulent monsoonal weather was exceptionally dangerous; between July 1942 and the end of the war 600 planes and 1,000 aircrew were lost delivering 650,000 tons of supplies.

In April 1944 the Japanese began a major offensive – the Ichigo offensive, with 620,000 troops – to overrun the Allied airfields in southern China. The warlord and Nationalist armies were no matches for the Japanese, who by December were threatening Kunming and Chungking. By this stage the new B-29 Superfortresses that had been conducting raids against southern Japan with limited success had been withdrawn to India. The Japanese called off their offensive, and in January 1945 the Chinese mounted counteroffensives that pushed the Japanese back to the South China Sea. During 1944 the Japanese had been forced to transfer troops to the Pacific, and in 1945 to Manchuria to meet an increasing Russian threat. By this time, "Vinegar Joe" Stilwell, frustrated by Chiang Kai-shek's deviousness and corruption in the Nationalist army, had been replaced by the more diplomatic Lieutenant-General Albert Wedemeyer. The war in China cost the lives of 1.3 million Chinese troops, not to mention the millions of civilians who died from famine, and tied down a million Japanese troops, but in reality it was a sideshow in a war that was won and lost in the Pacific.

The submarine campaign

The American submarine campaign against Japanese merchant shipping played a decisive role in strangling the Japanese home economy and starving the forward areas of reinforcements, supplies, and equipment. Japan relied heavily on its merchant marine – the world's third largest after those of Britain and the USA. Its merchant ships carried oil, rubber, tin, rice, and other raw materials from southeast Asia to the home islands, and also transported troops, supplies, and equipment to Japanese forces deployed in hundreds of islands from Sumatra to the Solomons and the central Pacific. In December 1941 the USA resolved on a policy of unrestricted submarine warfare. About 50 submarines, based initially at Hawaii and Fremantle (Australia), attacked Japanese merchant shipping and soon began to have a noticeable effect.

For the first two years, malfunctioning torpedoes hindered the American submarine campaign. Nonetheless, during 1943 Vice-Admiral Charles Lockwood, at Pearl Harbor, commanded a successful campaign against Japanese merchant shipping, and also supported the US surface fleet by sinking several Japanese carriers. The Americans had broken the ciphers used by the Japanese to route their merchant convoys, and the American submarines were usually lying in wait.

The USA's submarines were handled with great enterprise. By contrast, the Japanese submarine force usually operated in cooperation with its surface fleet and did not conduct a concerted campaign against Allied merchant shipping. It undertook small nuisance raids against the west coast of the USA, along the coast of Australia and even as far west as Madagascar, but these attacks did not cause heavy Allied losses. As it became more difficult to resupply forward Japanese positions, submarines were used to transport men and supplies – a wasteful use of a valuable strike weapon.

At the beginning of 1944 the Japanese had 4.1 million tons of merchant shipping, excluding tankers; by the end of the year this was down to 2 million tons. In September 1944, 700,000 tons of shipping were transporting oil; four months later this had been reduced to 200,000 tons, and during 1945 Japan imported virtually no oil. By the end of 1944 the submarine war was almost over. Japanese ships had been driven from the high seas and instead hugged the coast of China and the waters around Japan.

During the war, American submarines sank nearly 1,300 Japanese merchant ships, as well as one battleship, eight carriers, and 11 cruisers. The Americans lost 52 submarines from a total force of 288. During the same period, the Japanese lost 128 of their available 200 submarines, although many of these were not engaged in combat operations.

The importance of the American submarine campaign is sometimes overlooked, but after the war the former Japanese Prime Minister, General Tojo, admitted that there were three reasons for the American victory: the USA's ability to keep strong naval task forces at sea for months on end; the leap-frogging offensive that bypassed Japanese garrisons; and the destruction of Japanese shipping by American submarines.

Planning the final campaigns

In mid-October 1944 the Japanese East Asia Co-prosperity Sphere was still largely intact. After nearly three years of war, the Allies had made relatively minor progress, even though the Japanese had been defeated in important battles. In northern Burma, the Allies had not yet opened the road to China. Farther south, almost all of the Netherlands East Indies, the Philippines, Malaya, and Indochina remained in Japanese hands. In the Pacific, the Marianas were being rapidly developed to take B-29 Superfortresses for the bombing campaign against Japan. But American bombers had not reached Tokyo since April 1942.

Although much of Japan's empire was still intact, the signs were ominous. The Japanese navy had been decimated, and it had lost large numbers of irreplaceable naval aircraft and pilots. To the south, the Japanese seemed powerless to stop MacArthur's advance. In Burma they were in retreat. Their merchant fleet was suffering crippling losses to American submarines. Senior army and navy leaders in Tokyo now knew that they had no hope

of victory. Yet equally, there was no thought of surrender, and they hoped that somehow they might still resist their attackers, perhaps obtaining a negotiated peace. The Allies were never likely to contemplate such an outcome.

The shape of the last year of the Pacific War was set at important meetings in Quebec and Washington in mid-September and early October 1944. At Quebec, Churchill, Roosevelt, and their Chiefs of Staff agreed that Mountbatten's Southeast Asia Command would undertake an offensive into Burma; its forces were eventually to invade Malaya and capture Singapore. The Americans accepted Britain's offer of a major fleet to operate with the US navy in the Pacific. The Americans, however, would conduct the remainder of the offensives, including the strategic bombing campaign against Japan, and the landing at Mindanao in the southern Philippines. Eventually the Allies would have to invade Japan, and after the end of the war in Europe the Soviet Union would invade Manchuria to hold down the large Japanese army there.

In the midst of the conference came further news from the Pacific. Between September 7 and 14, Halsey's carrier force struck vigorously at Yap, the Palaus, Mindanao, and the central Philippines. He reported excitedly to Nimitz that he had found little opposition in the Philippines; he believed that Yap, Talaud, and Sarangani could be bypassed and the forces scheduled for those islands used against Leyte in the central Philippines. On September 15 the US Joint Chiefs approved a landing by MacArthur's forces on Leyte, beginning on October 20. The landing on Mindanao was abandoned.

Finally, in Washington on October 3, the Joint Chiefs resolved an issue that had been simmering for six months, namely whether the USA should invade Luzon or Formosa (now Taiwan). It was agreed that MacArthur's forces would invade Luzon on December 20, 1944. Nimitz's Central Pacific Command would seize Iwo Jima in late January 1945, and would move on to Okinawa on March 1.

Task Group 38.3 of Halsey's Third Fleet returning to its base in the Palaus after air strikes against Japanese airfields in the Philippines in September 1944. The two carriers, followed by three fast battleships and four cruisers, illustrate the growing power of the US Pacific Fleet. (US National Archives)

Liberation of the Philippines

The invasion force for Leyte consisted of the US Seventh Fleet under Vice-Admiral Thomas Kinkaid and four infantry divisions of the US Sixth Army, commanded by the veteran professional soldier General Walter Krueger. Admiral Halsey's powerful US Third Fleet, with 16 carriers, provided support. The total force numbered 700 ships and some 160,000 men. The troops landed on Leyte on October 20, 1944 and initially met only light opposition.

Meanwhile, the Japanese navy, under the tactical command of Vice-Admiral Ozawa

Jizaburo, converged on the US fleet. Ozawa lured Halsey north away from the landing area while he sent two striking forces into the Leyte Gulf. The subsequent battle, beginning on October 24, was the largest and one of the most decisive naval battles in history. With the battle in the balance, the commander of one of the Japanese striking forces, Vice-Admiral Kurita, called off the engagement and retired. By October 26 the Japanese had lost four carriers, three battleships, nine cruisers, and 10 destroyers. The Japanese navy never recovered from this defeat. Before the landing, the US navy had destroyed over 500 Japanese carrier- and land-based aircraft.

Defeated at sea, but aware of the danger if the Americans gained a foothold in the Philippines, the Japanese high command mounted a desperate counteroffensive. They were aided by the Americans' failure to

Philippines operations, October 20, 1944–July 1945

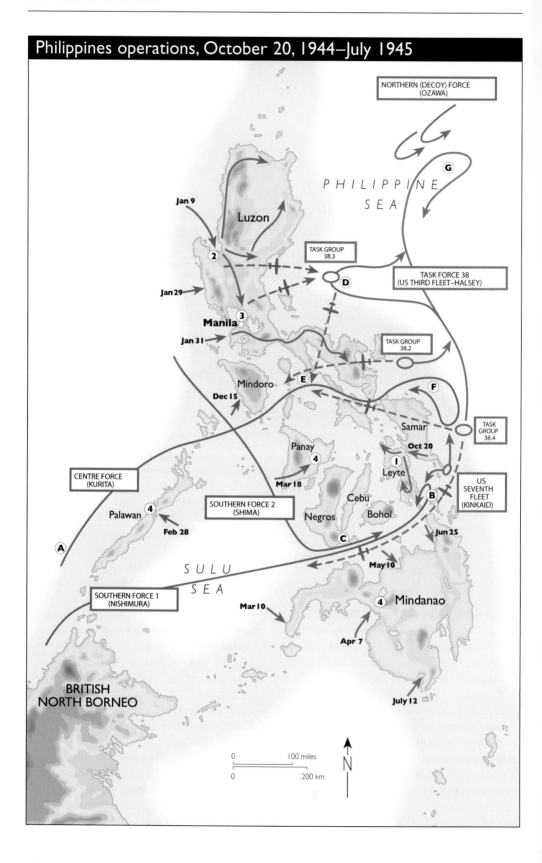

LEFT Map
Landings and land operations
1. October 20, 1944, US Sixth Army (Krueger), with four divisions, lands at Leyte. Three more divisions are deployed before the island is secured in December
2. January 9, 1945, US Sixth Army, with four divisions, lands at Lingayen Gulf. Six more divisions are landed during the battle for Luzon. The main fighting ceases in June, although pockets of Japanese remain
3. February 4–March 3, 1945, battle for Manila
4. February–July 1945, US Eighth Army (Eichelberger), with five divisions, conducts operations in the southern Philippines. They conduct over 50 landings, 14 of which are medium to large operations

Battle of Leyte Gulf
A October 23, 1944, US submarines sink two Japanese cruisers and damage one

B October 24, 1944, Japanese Southern Force 1 (Nishimura) enters Surigao Strait and is engaged by US Seventh Fleet (Kinkaid). Only one Japanese ship survives
C October 24, 1944, Japanese Southern Force 2 (Shima) withdraws without entering Surigao Strait
D October 24, 1944 the carrier, USS *Princeton*, sunk by Japanese land-based aircraft
E October 24, 1944, US air strikes sink Japanese battleship and damage a cruiser
F October 25, 1944, Japanese Center Force (Kurita) retreats back through San Bernadino Strait after losing two cruisers. The US lost two escort carriers, two destroyers, and a destroyer escort
G October 25, 1944, Halsey's Third Fleet engages Northern (Decoy) Force (Ozawa) before withdrawing to meet the southern threats

General Douglas MacArthur, Commander-in-Chief of the Southwest Pacific Area, wading ashore at Leyte, Philippines, in October 1944. Whatever the political and strategic merits might have been in liberating the Philippines, MacArthur had made it a personal crusade, vowing, after he arrived in Australia in March 1942: "I shall return." He was a master of public relations, using his extravagantly worded communiqués to engender support for his strategic plans. (US National Archives)

maintain air superiority: many American carriers had withdrawn for other tasks and the captured airfields on Leyte were in such poor condition that only a few aircraft could use them. The Japanese were therefore relatively free to send convoys of reinforcements to Leyte. Advancing cautiously from its beachhead, the US Sixth Army soon met strong resistance from skillful and determined Japanese troops. In a daring but uncoordinated attack, Japanese paratroops dropped on to the American airfields but were destroyed in a four-day battle. Eventually the Americans deployed seven divisions before concluding the hard-fought campaign successfully on December 25. The Japanese lost some 56,000 men. The Sixth Army had almost 3,000 killed and 10,000 wounded before it was relieved by Lieutenant-General Robert Eichelberger's US Eighth Army.

On January 9, 1945 the Sixth Army landed at Lingayen Gulf on the main Philippines island of Luzon. Attacked by Japanese kamikaze (suicide) planes, the Americans had 25 ships sunk or damaged, but 175,000 men were put ashore. The subsequent land campaign against a Japanese army of 260,000 under General Yamashita was the second largest conducted by the US army in the entire war, after that in northwest Europe in 1944–45. The Sixth Army deployed ten divisions and the campaign involved tank battles, amphibious landings, parachute drops, and guerrilla warfare. More than 100,000 Filipinos, 16,000 Japanese, and 1,000 Americans died in the two-week battle for the shattered city of Manila. By the end of June the Luzon campaign was over. The Sixth Army had lost 8,000 killed and 30,000 wounded. The Japanese had lost 190,000.

The Sixth Army now began to prepare for the invasion of Japan. Meanwhile, the Eighth Army undertook a series of amphibious operations throughout the southern Philippines to eliminate large pockets of Japanese. These operations helped liberate extensive areas but did not contribute directly to the defeat of Japan.

The Australian campaigns

The same criticism can be levelled at the Australian army's final campaigns. From October 1944, troops of the First Australian Army began relieving American divisions on Bougainville, New Britain, and the north coast of New Guinea. In New Britain, the Australians conducted a containment operation, and at the end of the war the Japanese garrison at Rabaul was found to number almost 70,000 army and naval personnel.

The Australian commander, General Blamey, argued, however, that Australia had a duty to liberate its own territory. Therefore, on Bougainville the 2nd Australian Corps began a slow and careful offensive, which was still proceeding at the end of the war. In New

Guinea the 6th Division captured Wewak, driving the Japanese into the mountains.

MacArthur was at best lukewarm about the justification for these offensives, but he enthusiastically ordered the 1st Australian Corps, under Lieutenant-General Sir Leslie Morshead, to conduct operations in Borneo. The first of these began on May 1, 1945 with the seizure of Tarakan. Next, on June 10 the 9th Australian Division landed on Labuan Island and at Brunei. Blamey was now more wary and he opposed the landing of the 7th Division at Balikpapan. MacArthur warned the Australian government that to cancel the operation would disorganize Allied strategic plans; the government approved the landing. In truth, MacArthur wanted to show the Dutch government that he had attempted to recover part of its territory. The landing on July 1 was the last amphibious operation of the war. In the campaigns of late 1944 and 1945 the Australians lost more than 1,500 killed, but Japan did not surrender one minute earlier as a result.

The end in Burma

In December 1944 the British–Indian Fourteenth Army, under the popular and pragmatic General Slim, crossed the Chindwin River, and by January 1945 it had reached the Irrawaddy River in central Burma. British, Chinese, and American forces in northern Burma advanced south and on January 22 the Burma Road, linking India and China, was opened.

With more than six divisions in a force numbering 260,000, Slim continued his offensive southward toward Rangoon. He was opposed by four Japanese divisions, together totalling some 20,000 emaciated and poorly equipped defenders. However, British and Indian troops landed from the sea and by air, and took Rangoon on May 3. The Japanese army in Burma had been crushed. Faced with a possible invasion of India, the British had had no alternative but to fight in Burma. It had been a hard-fought war over three years; 190,000 Japanese died. Burma was liberated,

A British patrol at the Sittang River in the final stages of the Burma campaign. After the capture of Rangoon, the British forces faced a force of 110,000 Japanese troops, but short of supplies they were generally ineffective. (The Art Archive/Imperial War Museum)

British pride was restored, and Japanese forces had been tied down. But in strategic terms the 1945 Burma campaign had only a marginal effect on the outcome of the war.

The way was now clear for the British to prepare for the invasion of Malaya. Organized by Mountbatten's Southeast Asia Command, the landing (Operation Zipper) took place in September 1945, after Japan had surrendered.

Iwo Jima and Okinawa

Iwo Jima was a key location: as long as the Japanese occupied it, the B-29s from the Marianas had to fly a dog-leg on their way to Japan with consequent expenditure of fuel and reduction in bomb loads. Once it was captured, long-range fighters stationed there could accompany the B-29s on their raids. Furthermore, Iwo Jima would provide an emergency landing place for returning bombers and, since it was traditional Japanese territory, its loss would be a severe psychological blow to the Japanese.

If Luzon was the largest battle of the Pacific War, Iwo Jima was the bloodiest. Only 5 miles (8 km) long, the island had been turned into a formidable fortress with underground bunkers, tunnels, and well-concealed heavy artillery. All civilians had been evacuated to Japan. The Japanese commander, Lieutenant-General Kuribayashi Tadamichi, was determined not to waste his men in suicidal attacks but grimly to defend every yard. Expecting a fight to the death, he commanded his force skillfully. On February 19, 1945 two US Marine divisions, under Major-General Harry Schmidt, landed under cover of gunfire from seven battleships. But the Marines soon found that there was no place to escape the constant Japanese artillery and machine gun fire. Each Japanese strongpoint had to be attacked separately, the best weapons being artillery, tanks, and flamethrowers.

A photograph of the Marines' raising of an American flag on Mount Suribachi early in the campaign became one of the most famous war photographs. But more than 100,000 Marines and naval personnel were landed before they secured the island in late March. Of the commanders of the 24 battalions that had come ashore in the first landing, 19 were killed or wounded. The Marines had lost 6,821 killed and almost 20,000 wounded. The 21,000 Japanese defenders died almost to a

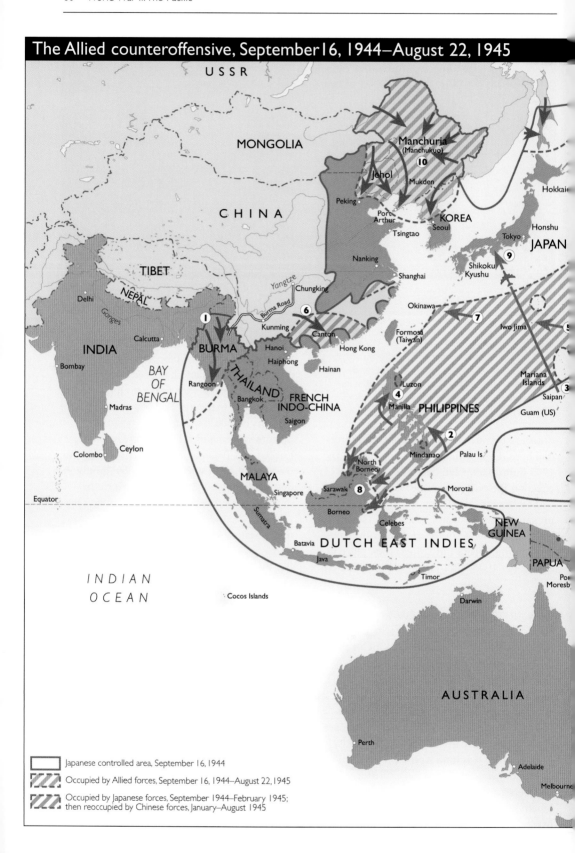

The Allied counteroffensive, September 16, 1944–August 22, 1945

USSR

MONGOLIA

Manchuria
(Manchukuo)
10

Jehol

Mukden

CHINA

Peking

Hokkaido

Port
Arthur

Tsingtao

KOREA
Seoul

Honshu

Tokyo
JAPAN

Nanking

Shanghai

Shikoku
Kyushu

9

TIBET

Yangtze
Chungking

Okinawa

NEPAL

Burma Road

6

Formosa
(Taiwan)

Iwo Jima

7

5

Delhi

Ganges

1

Kunming

Canton

INDIA

Calcutta

BURMA

Hanoi

Hong Kong

Mariana
Islands

3

Bombay

Haiphong

Hainan

Saipan

BAY
OF
BENGAL

Rangoon

THAILAND

Luzon

4

Guam (US)

Madras

Bangkok

FRENCH
INDO-CHINA

Manila

PHILIPPINES

Saigon

2

Colombo

Ceylon

Mindanao

Palau Is

North
Borneo

MALAYA

Singapore

Sarawak

8

Morotai

Equator

Sumatra

Borneo

Celebes

NEW
GUINEA

Batavia   DUTCH EAST INDIES

PAPUA

Java

Timor

Port
Moresby

INDIAN
OCEAN

Cocos Islands

Darwin

AUSTRALIA

Perth

Adelaide

Melbourne

☐ Japanese controlled area, September 16, 1944

▨ Occupied by Allied forces, September 16, 1944–August 22, 1945

▨ Occupied by Japanese forces, September 1944–February 1945;
then reoccupied by Chinese forces, January–August 1945

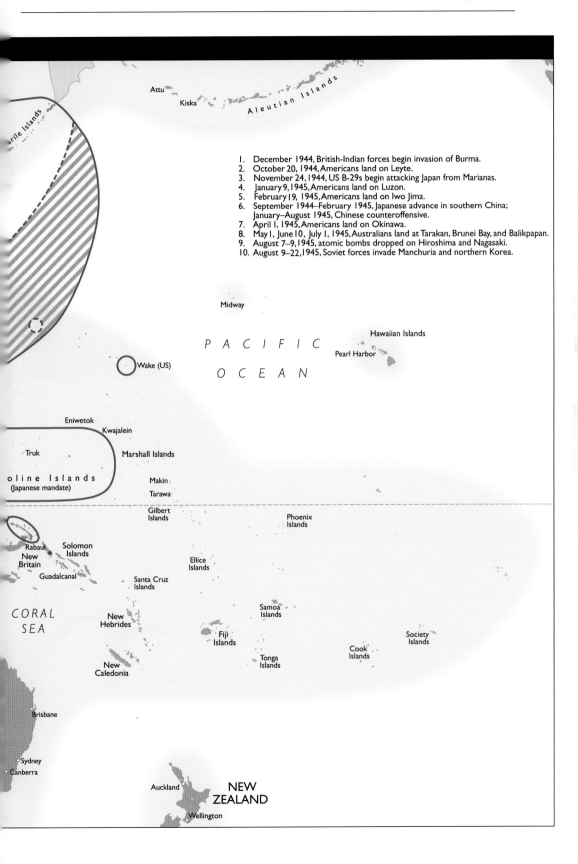

1. December 1944, British-Indian forces begin invasion of Burma.
2. October 20, 1944, Americans land on Leyte.
3. November 24, 1944, US B-29s begin attacking Japan from Marianas.
4. January 9, 1945, Americans land on Luzon.
5. February 19, 1945, Americans land on Iwo Jima.
6. September 1944–February 1945, Japanese advance in southern China;
    January–August 1945, Chinese counteroffensive.
7. April 1, 1945, Americans land on Okinawa.
8. May 1, June 10, July 1, 1945, Australians land at Tarakan, Brunei Bay, and Balikpapan.
9. August 7–9, 1945, atomic bombs dropped on Hiroshima and Nagasaki.
10. August 9–22, 1945, Soviet forces invade Manchuria and northern Korea.

American naval landing craft unloading fuel and supplies at Okinawa on April 13, 1945. The US Tenth Army took two and a half months to secure the islands. The army's casualties were more than 7,000 killed. The Japanese had 70,000 killed with at least 80,000 Okinawan civilians killed. (US National Archives)

man. Marine Lieutenant-General Holland Smith, commanding the land operation, said, "This fight is the toughest we've run across in 168 years."

For the attack on Okinawa on April 1, the Americans amassed a huge naval force of 1,300 ships, including 18 battleships, 40 aircraft carriers, and 200 destroyers. They were also supported by the British Pacific Fleet. The Japanese resisted fiercely, as they considered the Ryukyu Islands to be part of their home territory. The US Tenth Army, commanded by Lieutenant-General Simon Buckler, with two Marine divisions and three army divisions, put nearly 250,000 men ashore, lost 7,600 killed, and took until June 22 to secure the island.

At sea the battle was equally fierce with the Japanese launching 1,900 kamikaze missions. Admiral Spruance's US Fifth Fleet had 36 ships sunk and 368 damaged. Almost 5,000 American sailors were killed. The giant Japanese battleship *Yamato* set sail from the Inland Sea but was caught by US planes. It sank with the loss of 3,000 sailors.

The seizure of Okinawa tended to make all campaigns fought to the south strategically irrelevant, but the outcome of the battle was deeply troubling to the Americans. On May 25, MacArthur and Nimitz were ordered to prepare for an invasion of Japan, with the first landing on Kyushu on November 1. The Marines and army had suffered 35 percent casualties on Okinawa. On that basis, there could be more than a quarter of a million casualties in Kyushu.

Strategic bombing

The strategic bombing offensive was based on the employment of the new B-29 Superfortress bombers. Initially, from June 1944, they conducted raids from China, but without great success. Then, from November, they started operating from the Marianas, still with limited effect. In March 1945 the young, cigar-chomping Major-General Curtis Le May, commanding the Twentieth Air Force, changed tactics from high-level daylight raids against specific targets to low-level night attacks with incendiaries against area targets.

The first attack on Tokyo, on March 9–10, succeeded beyond expectations. The Americans lost 14 of the 334 planes taking part. About 15 square miles (40 km^2) of the city were burnt out, more than 80,000 inhabitants were killed and 40,000 wounded, and 250,000 buildings were destroyed. Before the end of the month Nagoya, Osaka, and Kobe were similarly attacked. As more aircraft joined his command, Le May stepped up the offensive.

The strategic bombing campaign complemented the Allied blockade of the Japanese home islands. By the end of 1944 the American submarine campaign had restricted Japanese merchant shipping to the routes around Japan and Korea, and US army and navy aircraft attacked even the smallest coastal

B-29 Superfortresses from the US Twentieth Air Force conducting a daylight raid over Yokohama on May 29, 1945. Their escorts shot down 26 Japanese fighters. By July 1945, 60 percent of the areas of Japan's 60 larger cities and towns had been burnt out. (Imperial War Museum)

ships. Then in March 1945 the Twentieth Air Force began the systematic mining of Japanese home waters to prevent the transportation of food and raw materials from China, Korea, and Manchuria. In March 1945, 320,000 tons of shipping was using the main Japanese port of Kobe; by July the figure was down to 44,000 tons. The mining operation was the most effective single element in the final blockade against Japan.

The blockade had a devastating effect on the Japanese economy and public. Millions of homeless lived in shanties. Hunger and disease were widespread. Civilian morale plummeted and the police had to clamp down ruthlessly on defeatist talk. A secret report to the Diet in June 1945 admitted that in view of the worsening food shortage the war could not be maintained beyond the spring of 1946. The blockade also had a severe effect on Japan's ability to fight the war, restricting its capacity to replace military equipment and, through lack of fuel, reducing its ability to deploy planes and ships. But the government and military leaders were determined to fight on. Suicide units of different descriptions were formed to counter the expected Allied landings.

Thomas Currie Derrick, an Australian soldier

Like most American and Australian soldiers in the Pacific War, Thomas Currie Derrick was a child of the Great Depression. With his limited education, army service gave him opportunities that would never have been available in civilian life. Although he was to become one of the Australian army's most courageous and accomplished soldiers, the story of his life is otherwise representative of the thousands of young men who volunteered "for the duration."

Born in Adelaide, South Australia, in 1914, Tom Derrick left school at 14, but could only find odd jobs. As the Depression deepened, aged 16, he rode with some mates on their bikes about 140 miles (225 km) to the Murray River irrigation area, seeking itinerant work in the vineyards and orchards. Cheerful and hardworking, he was often up to mischief, but enjoyed football, boxing, gambling, and the company of his mates, who gave him the nickname "Diver." By 1939 he had gained steady employment in a vineyard and was able to marry his long-time sweetheart, Beryl.

Newly married, Derrick hesitated to volunteer for the army when war was declared in September 1939, but loyal to his country, and also to his mates who had joined, he persuaded Beryl, who eventually relented. Like others, he was influenced by Germany's invasion of France in May 1940, and the next month he enlisted in the 2/48th Battalion, then being raised in Adelaide.

Used to hard living, Derrick thrived on army life, but he found discipline difficult to accept. The battalion sailed for the Middle East in November, but stopped for a week at Perth. Confined to ship after going absent for sightseeing, he was taunted by another soldier, who punched him. In a letter home Derrick wrote, "Got clocked last night, broke teeth and cut lip. I then got stuck into him,

made a real job of him. On another [charge] now for fighting." Although only 5 ft 7 in (170 cm) tall, Derrick was strong and wiry, with plenty of fighting experience. The commanding officer fined him 30 shillings.

Between April and October 1941 the battalion – part of the 9th Australian Division – helped defend the besieged port of Tobruk, in Libya. Derrick was soon leading his section and was promoted to corporal. He was recommended for a Military Medal. It was richly deserved but was not awarded.

Back in action in July 1942, the battalion attacked a German–Italian position near El Alamein. Derrick's leadership was inspirational. Hurling grenades, he personally destroyed three machine gun posts and captured more than a hundred prisoners. When the Germans counterattacked, he destroyed two enemy tanks and restored the position. He was awarded the Distinguished Conduct Medal and promoted to sergeant.

Derrick was also in the thick of the fighting at El Alamein in late October. Those present thought that he should have earned the Victoria Cross. In a week of savage combat the battalion lost more than 400 men. Derrick had been slightly wounded.

The 9th Division returned to Australia, and Derrick enjoyed his leave with Beryl in Adelaide in February 1943. Then the battalion took the long train journey to the Atherton Tableland in north Queensland, where it began intensive jungle training in preparation for operations against the Japanese. Valuable lessons from the 1942 Papuan campaign were incorporated into the training, and platoons learned to patrol silently in the jungle.

The battalion also practiced amphibious operations with the US 532nd Engineer Shore and Boat Battalion. Derrick wrote, "Spent morning embarking and debarking –

After almost three years of soldiering, including grim battles in the Middle East, Sergeant Tom Derrick, and his battalion's other veterans, had the qualities of long-service professional soldiers. Back in Australia in early 1943 the battalion retrained for a different war against the Japanese. (Australian War Memorial)

find there is little to it and should not take many attempts to become really efficient."

Lieutenant Murray Farquar, an officer in Derrick's battalion, recalled that Derrick met a young American soldier from Wisconsin, still in his teens, from the Shore and Boat Battalion. They adjourned to a hotel, where civilians and soldiers were

elbowing their way forward to replenish their glasses. In turn this young Yank pressed forward. He became the target of what was, at first, only good-humoured banter. One or two louts soon became vicious. Finally, backed up by a team of six or seven, one spat out, "If you think you'll get out of here, Yank, without a few teeth smashed in, you've got another thing coming." This aggressor was a real lump of a man. Quickly Diver sized things up. Stepping in front of his new mate, he stated: "Well, you'll have to go through me first." No histrionics, just a quiet

statement of intent. Staring this mob out, he held his ground … There were a few rumbles, they shrugged shoulders, and turned back to their drinking … finishing his beer, Diver exclaimed, "Well, come on Yank. We'll try another pub." The confrontation was over; Diver had won yet another ardent admirer.

Derrick merely wrote in his diary, "Nought to do today … Murray Farquar and myself went into Cairns, teamed up with a Yank and had a most enjoyable day."

In August 1943 the battalion sailed for Milne Bay in New Guinea. After arriving, Derrick wrote in his diary:

Slept on some very wet ground and was surprised to find I had a very comfortable and dry sleep. Seen my first glimpse of the Fuzzy Wuzzy's who appear very friendly. The camp is situated midst a huge coconut plantation, my first effort to climb a palm ended at 30 feet (9 m). But I think I can master it. The average height seems to be almost 45 feet (14 m).

The battalion landed near Lae in September, and by November was attacking the heights of Sattelberg, overlooking Finschhafen. The Allied advance hinged on clearing both sides of the Vitiaz Strait. Sattelberg dominated the mainland side. On November 17 the battalion led the brigade attack, but by November 24 the attack was grinding to a halt, the battalion suffering casualties. Late that day Derrick was leading the advance platoon when the battalion commander ordered a withdrawal. Derrick appealed to his company commander, "Forget the CO. Just give me twenty minutes and we'll have this place."

It was a one-man front up an almost vertical incline covered in jungle. In peacetime the climb is barely possible using both hands and feet. Covered by his platoon members, Derrick alone clambered up the cliff, holding on with one hand, throwing grenades with another, pausing to fire his rifle. He cleared 10 machine gun posts before, at dusk, he reached an open patch, just short of the crest. Fifteen Japanese dead

Troops of the 2/48th Australian Infantry Battalion moving forward with a tank of the 1st Army Tank Battalion for the attack on Sattelberg in November 1943. Tanks were used for blasting Japanese defensive positions. (Australian War Memorial)

remained on the spur. Derrick's platoon occupied the area. That night the remaining Japanese withdrew. Awarded the Victoria Cross, Derrick said that the achievement was due mainly to his mates.

When the battalion returned to Australia for leave and more training, Derrick attended an officer-training course. Although lacking formal education, he had a great thirst for knowledge. In November 1944 he returned as a lieutenant to his battalion on the Atherton Tableland. Friends thought that he should not have returned; after three campaigns he had "done his bit." But he merely replied, "My boys are back there, I must be with them."

On May 1, 1945, the 2/48th Battalion was part of the Australian landing on Tarakan, Borneo. The Japanese fiercely resisted

attempts to clear the island. On May 23 Derrick's platoon led the assault on a position known as Freda. One soldier recalled: "At Diver's signal, we smashed forward. Grenades burst among us. Diver was everywhere, encouraging, shouting orders, pressing us on." Those present thought that his actions were worthy of a bar to his Victoria Cross. The Australians took the knoll but expected a Japanese counterattack that night. At about 3:00 am a Japanese machine gun fired down a track where Derrick was sleeping. He sat up to assess the direction of the fire. Another burst of fire struck him in the abdomen. "I've been hit. I think its curtains," he said. "I've copped it in the fruit and nuts" (rhyming slang for "the guts"). He insisted that the other wounded be evacuated first and died the next day.

Apart from his extraordinary feats on the battlefield, Derrick was typical of the Australian soldier who enlisted in the early years of the war. He learned his trade of soldiering against the Germans and Italians in the Middle East and then returned to deal

Men of the 2/48th Battalion gather for the graveside funeral of Lieutenant Derrick, conducted by the battalion's chaplain on Tarakan Island, May 26, 1945. Shortly before he died Derrick told the priest, "Give me the works, father, I know I've had it." (Australian War Memorial)

with the Japanese. With few advantages in life, he had come to rely on his mates and applied himself to any task. His ever present grin and outgoing leadership masked a sensitive and reflective side. He collected butterflies, composed poetry, kept a diary, and wrote regularly and frequently to his wife. After the war he would have happily returned to the Murray River fruit blocks.

Raised as a Salvationist, Derrick was not overtly religious. In the Middle East, in February 1942, he wrote, "Changed my church today, went to Catholic parade – doubt if I'm improved any." During his evacuation on Tarakan, he asked a friend to get the priest so that he could "bring on the hocus pocus." Cheerful to the end, he had done his duty as he saw it. It was men like him who made the Australian army a formidable force in the southwest Pacific.

A clash of cultures and races

The Pacific War was a clash of cultures and races – not only between East and West, but also between the Japanese and other Asian peoples. It brought death to millions, and hardship and misery to hundreds of millions of people across east and southeast Asia. Yet the civilian population of the USA remained largely untouched by the war.

Japan

In Japan, by the time of Pearl Harbor, an authoritarian government was already exercising tight control over the economy. Soon, as shipping was diverted to military purposes, supplies of food and other goods became restricted. Except for the ineffectual Doolittle raid in April 1942, Japan was free from enemy attack until June 1944, and even these attacks did little damage until 1945. Nonetheless, as the Allied blockade took effect, life became increasingly hard. Black market prices for all manner of goods soared. In 1943 about 11,000 Tokyo shops closed their doors for lack of merchandise or staff. In September 1943 unmarried women under 25 were conscripted to a labor volunteer corps and by the following year 14 million women were wage earners.

By the last year of the war, most Japanese civilians were hungry, eating anything that would grow – thistle, mugwort, and chickweed – or anything that could be caught, such as dogs and cats. Working hours became longer and workers became listless through malnutrition and illness. Japanese society was being strangled. Youths were indoctrinated to serve the Empire and the nation, and young boys expected to die for their country. The age for military conscription was lowered to 18, but eventually boys were permitted to volunteer at 15.

Dissent was suppressed. The military police – the Kempeitai – who kept law and order in the military, turned their attention to civilians. The special higher police – the Tokku, equivalent to the German Gestapo – arrested critics of government policy. The editor of a respected magazine was arrested by a Tokku inspector who told him that he knew the editor was not a communist, "But if you intend to be stubborn ... we'll just set you up as a communist. We can kill communists."

Japanese cities, with thousands of closely built houses of wood and paper, were particularly vulnerable to incendiary attacks. When the US Twentieth Air Force turned to low-level incendiary attacks in March 1945, the result was devastating. By the end of July nearly 500,000 Japanese had been killed, some 2 million buildings had been destroyed, and 9–13 million people were homeless, living in shanties.

Imperial General Headquarters initiated plans to defend the homeland. In June 1945 the People's Volunteer Combat Corps was formed for men between 15 and 60, and women between 17 and 40. Most were armed with only spears and staves. Government propagandists advocated "The Glorious Death of One Hundred Million" to defend the nation. By the time of the surrender in September 1945, Japanese society was on it knees, its people mentally and physically exhausted.

One constant feature was the authority and position of Emperor Hirohito, who was seen as the symbol of Japanese nationalism. The standard view is that Hirohito was a constitutional monarch with no control over the direction of his government. Nonetheless, as a nationalist he supported prosecution of the war once the decision had been made.

Korea

Although the Japanese populace suffered severely and its economy was shattered, Japan survived by ruthlessly exploiting its colonies – Manchukuo, Korea, and Taiwan – and the conquered lands of China and southeast Asia. Korea was treated harshly. The Korean language was banned from schools and Koreans were ordered to change their names to Japanese ones. In 1942 Koreans began to be conscripted into the Japanese army and civilian workers were sent overseas. More than 650,000 Koreans worked in Japan, where 60,000 died. Tens of thousands of Korean women were forced to work as "comfort women" in Japanese army brothels in southeast Asia and the Pacific. Korea was stripped of its rice production and anything else that could be used for war purposes.

China

Life in wartime China was perhaps even harder than in Korea, as the Japanese army made war on the civilian population, conducting "three all" punishment operations – kill all, burn all, loot all. In 1937 China had an estimated population of 480 million, 85 percent living in rural areas. In response to the Japanese offensives, about 12 million Chinese migrated west, away from the Japanese, suffering much misery on the journey, but millions more remained under Japanese rule, where they either voluntarily collaborated or were compelled to do so. In 1943 a famine in Honan Province, caused by drought and grain requisitions by Nationalist and provincial authorities, took hundreds of thousands of lives. Whether under Japanese or Nationalist rule, Chinese peasants suffered from rice requisitions, conscription, taxes, and corruption. It is not possible to determine how many Chinese died as a result of the war. Chinese military casualties exceeded 5 million killed and wounded. Perhaps between 10 and 20 million civilians died from starvation and disease. Both Chiang Kai-shek's Nationalists and Mao

Tse-tung's Communists bided their time, waiting until the end of the war before they turned on each other.

Nationalism and exploitation in southeast Asia

For much of the war, the Japanese tried to maintain the fiction that the countries of southeast Asia were its allies in a war against the Western Imperial powers. In November 1943 General Tojo presided in Tokyo over a conference of the Greater East Asia Co-prosperity Sphere with representatives from China, Manchukuo, Thailand, Burma, Free India, and the Philippines. "It is an incontrovertible fact," he said, "that the nations of Greater East Asia are bound in every respect by ties of an inseparable relationship." Jose Laurel, President of the Philippines, recently granted independence by Japan, replied that no power could "stop or delay the acquisition by the one billion Orientals of the free and untrammelled right and opportunity to shape their own destiny." Japan ruled the southeast Asian countries harshly, with little consideration for their people, even though they generally arranged nominally independent governments in them. In the Philippines, some former members of the Philippines army (supported by American special forces teams) conducted guerrilla operations. But most Filipinos tried to accommodate their new rulers, while some Filipinos collaborated with the Japanese. In the hope that it might lessen resistance to their rule, in 1943 Japan granted independence to the Philippines. In September 1944 the Philippines declared war on the USA, but guerrillas continued to fight the Japanese, and the Philippines government-in-exile was restored when the Americans liberated the country.

As a reward for collaboration, Japan allowed Thailand to occupy the northern states of Malaya and later to take two Burmese states. Gradually, resistance groups and guerrilla organizations were formed to oppose the Japanese. To supply its forces in

Burma, between July 1942 and October 1943 the Japanese army built a railroad from Nong Pladuk in Thailand 260 miles (420 km) through mountainous jungle to Thanbyuzayat in Burma. In addition to Allied prisoners of war, more than 270,000 native laborers from Burma, Thailand, Malaya, and the Netherlands East Indies worked on the railway; about 90,000 perished.

In Burma the Japanese established a civilian Burmese government under Ba Maw, who declared war on the Allies in August 1943. The Burmese Independence Army, formed in December 1941, fought alongside the Japanese in the British retreat of 1942. It was later dissolved by the Japanese, who then formed the Burma National Army, commanded by Bo Ne Win. The Burmese Defence Minister, Aung San, and the Burmese National Army defected to the British in April 1945. The army changed its name to the Patriotic Burmese Forces and fought with the British army.

In general, the puppet regimes in Manchukuo, China, Burma, and the Philippines failed to win over their populations. Japan never looked upon the regimes as equal partners and the Japanese maintained their racial superiority. The seizure of rice and other raw materials and the exploitation of local labor soon alienated the local populations.

In Malaya, the Japanese had less success in establishing a local government. Malaya consisted of various states with different forms of government, and the population included almost equal numbers of Malays and Chinese, with smaller number of Indians. Malaya was a vital source of rubber and tin that was exploited by the Japanese. Members of the Malayan Communist Party, mostly Chinese, formed the Malay People's Anti-Japanese Army, which, assisted by British special forces operatives, conducted a guerrilla war against the Japanese. The Malayan Chinese were treated badly by the Japanese and those known to have contributed to the China Relief Fund were executed. Singapore was treated as a Japanese colony and thousands of local Chinese were massacred.

The Netherlands East Indies included Sumatra, Java, Dutch Borneo, Celebes, western Timor, the Moluccas, and Dutch New Guinea, and in 1940 had a population of about 70.5 million, 1 million being Chinese and 250,000 Dutch nationals. The Japanese interned the Dutch in harsh conditions and, as usual, were brutal toward the Chinese. Welcomed by the Indonesians as liberators, the Japanese were soon seen as severe overlords. Nationalist leaders, especially Achmad Sukarno and Mohammad Hatta, traded support for political concessions. In March 1943 they formed the Center of the People's Power (Putera) with Sukarno as chairman, and the following October a volunteer defense force was formed with Indonesian officers, trained by the Japanese; it was the forerunner of the Indonesian army. In March 1944 Putera was replaced by the People's Loyalty Association, and in September the Japanese government announced that it intended to prepare Indonesia for self-government. Work began on a constitution and on August 17, 1945 Sukarno proclaimed the independent state of Indonesia.

Japanese forces occupied French Indochina during 1940 and 1941. The French Governor-General, Vice-Admiral Jean Decoux, had 100,000 troops (mostly raised locally) but was ordered not to fight. Nominally he administered the country, but the Japanese garrison systematically stripped the country of rice, corn, coal, and rubber. Shortages caused immense hardships and in 1945 between 1.5 and 2 million people died of starvation in Tonkin.

A communist nationalist leader, Ho Chi Minh, formed the communist guerrilla organization the Viet Minh. Aided by the American Office of Strategic Services, it conducted operations from bases in China and established its own administration in northern Tonkin. The French authorities finally began to resist the Japanese, who seized control in March 1945. The Japanese then set up a puppet regime under the Emperor of Annam, Bao Dai. After the end of the war, Ho Chi Minh declared the formation of the Democratic Government of Vietnam.

India

India, the "jewel in the crown" of the British Empire, played a crucial role in the Pacific War. In 1941 it had a population of 318 million, and although it was underdeveloped and its people were poor, the country was so large that it still had the capacity to provide great quantities of manufactured goods and raw materials. The outbreak of the Pacific War accelerated the wartime mobilization, and the economy was directed primarily toward supporting the British–Indian operations in Burma.

The Bengal famine, in which probably more than 3 million perished, was caused by the failure of the harvest but was exacerbated by the war. It was no longer possible to import rice from Burma, transportation was disrupted by the needs of the war effort, and the Allies gave a low priority to shipping that might have brought food from overseas.

The Viceroy ruled India on behalf of the British government, although Indians held many senior administrative positions. The war brought increased agitation for independence. Some members of the Indian National Congress party saw the war as an opportunity to put pressure on Britain; others supported the war effort but with an eye to future independence. The Indian leader Mohandas Gandhi led a campaign of nonviolent civil disobedience. Congress was banned, its leaders were imprisoned, and Gandhi was interned. The government had to deploy troops to put down sporadic insurrections. Despite this disruption, through the provision of troops and munitions India made a huge contribution to the conduct of the war. Nonetheless, it became clear that the British Raj would not be able to continue much beyond the end of the war.

Initially the Japanese were not interested in the Indonesian independence movement, but only in exploiting the oil fields in Sumatra and Borneo, and obtaining other resources such as tin, rubber, coffee, and rice. With the Dutch removed from administration, however, the Japanese had to use Indonesian administrators, and enlisted the support of nationalist and Islamic leaders. Here Emperor Hirohito (left) meets the Indonesian nationalist leader, Sukarno (center). (Corbis)

After the fall of Singapore in February 1942, Japan encouraged the formation of the Indian National Army from among Indian army prisoners captured in Malaya and Singapore. Initially, 20,000 of the 60,000 prisoners volunteered, although the force was later reduced in size. In June 1943 the Indian revolutionary Subhas Chandra Bose, who had spent the early war years in Germany, took command and directed his force to assist the Japanese in their attack on India in 1944. Large numbers deserted to the British or surrendered during 1944 and 1945. The Indian National Army was never a credible fighting force, but its existence partly encouraged the Japanese to invade India in 1944.

USA

It is hard to separate the impact of the Pacific War on American life from the impact of the wider world war. The USA was propelled into war by the attack on Pearl Harbor, but Germany then declared war on the USA. A meeting between Churchill and Roosevelt and their military advisers in Washington in December 1941 and January 1942 (the Arcadia Conference) confirmed the decision of an earlier conference, that the Allies would concentrate their resources on beating Hitler first, before they turned to the Japanese. Admiral King, Chief of US Naval Operations, did not fully accept this decision, and in practice the USA committed large numbers of forces to the Pacific during 1942 and maintained the commitment throughout the war.

King was determined to take the fight to the Japanese as early as possible, but also the American public had a deep hatred of the Japanese for their sneak attack on Pearl Harbor. There were other imperatives. MacArthur's vow to return to the Philippines struck a chord with many Americans who wanted to recover their territory, and Roosevelt and the "China lobby" were determined to maintain aid to the Chinese Nationalist regime.

Distrust of the Japanese was reflected in the fear that 120,000 Japanese-Americans living in the West Coast states of California, Oregon, and Washington posed a security threat, and most were interned. In Hawaii, the 150,000 Japanese-Americans formed 37 percent of the population and were not interned. Japanese-Americans born in the USA (the Nisei) served with great valor in their own US army unit in Italy. Smaller groups of Nisei served as interpreters and translators in the Pacific theater.

While 16 million Americans served in the armed forces, and 290,000 died on all fronts (90,000 in the Pacific), the war caused considerably less misery to Americans than it did to the people of east and southeast Asia. In 1940 the USA had an unemployment rate of 15 percent and the nation was still recovering from the Great Depression. The expansion of American industry to meet the war demands of both its own armed forces and those of the Allies brought full employment with increased wages. Food production rose and, while there was price control and rationing, Americans ate more and healthier food during the war. Women joined the workforce in large numbers and there was better-paid work for minority groups and less skilled workers. Generally, the war increased the feeling of patriotism and national self-confidence.

Australia and New Zealand

Australia and New Zealand had been at war since September 1939. Both countries sent forces to fight in the Middle East, while at home they began gearing their economies to support the war effort. The outbreak of the Pacific War completely changed the complexion of these measures. With a population of only 7 million, Australia now found itself isolated from British support and faced with the possibility of Japanese invasion. In January 1942 Japanese forces landed in Australian mandate territory in New Guinea and the next month Japanese aircraft bombed the northern city of Darwin. Sporadic air raids continued until late 1943. Japanese submarines attacked coastal shipping.

Australia relied on Britain and the USA for the supply of sophisticated military equipment such as aircraft, but tried to become self-sufficient, and eventually constructed certain types of aircraft. With one in seven Australians in the armed forces, the supply of labor was a major problem, resulting in the conscription of labor, the employment of women, and even the use of Italian prisoners of war. Australia provided food and other supplies to its own armed forces, to the American forces in the Southwest Pacific Area, and to Britain. With stringent rationing and restrictions on travel, life was hard for Australian civilians.

Australia became a vast military base. Australian servicemen trained in northern areas before deploying for action, and casualties returned to Australian hospitals. Allied aircraft conducted operational raids from northern Australian airfields throughout the war, while Allied surface ships and submarines were based at Australian ports. The arrival of thousands of American servicemen in 1942 had a noticeable effect on both the military situation and Australian political and social life. The Prime Minister, John Curtin, looked to General MacArthur for advice on the strategic conduct of the war. Indeed, MacArthur and the Australian government joined forces to oppose the Allied policy of dealing with Hitler first. American requirements dictated the construction of airfields, roads, and other facilities around the country.

New Zealand too received an influx of American servicemen, although in smaller numbers and for a shorter period. It was further from the action and did not receive attacks on its territory. Otherwise, the war had similar effects to Australia, with rationing, labor shortages, and hardship.

Great Britain

Life for civilians in Britain was scarcely made more difficult by the outbreak of the Pacific War. Britain had mobilized its civilians more fully than any other combatant nation. Labor was conscripted, rationing was applied rigorously, and many cities suffered heavily from air attacks. The Pacific War created a new burden for the provision of troops, ships, and air force squadrons, but proportionally, these were far fewer than those needed in the European theater.

The outbreak of the Pacific War ensured that Britain would not lose the war with Germany. When told of the attack on Pearl Harbor, the Prime Minister, Churchill, understood that this brought the USA into the war. "So we had won after all," he wrote later. For most people in Britain, the Pacific War was out of sight and out of mind, except for the families of the servicemen involved. Those serving with the Fourteenth Army in Burma called it the "forgotten army." There were, however, fundamental differences with the USA over the conduct of the war. Roosevelt was determined that the war should not be fought to recover Europe's colonial empires. Britain, of course, was determined to regain Burma and Malaya.

Prisoners of war, and atrocities

As a clash of cultures and races, the war resulted in barbaric treatment of the 140,000–170,000 Allied prisoners captured in southeast Asia. Allied soldiers were also massacred on capture. For example, when the ship the *Vyner Brooke* was sunk off Banka Island in February 1942, the survivors, including nurses, soldiers, and civilians, struggled ashore, to be shot down by Japanese troops. Those Allied troops who survived the initial surrender endured three and half years of starvation, disease, slave labor, brutality, and torture. One in four died. The Japanese captured thousands of Chinese, Indians, Filipinos, and Indonesians serving with the European colonial armies and many of these were massacred soon after capture. But the majority were released within a few months.

American and Australian soldiers marching together in a Sydney street during a loan rally. With their sharp-looking uniforms, money, and access to unobtainable luxury goods, the Americans had an immediate effect on social life in the Australian cities; 10,000 Australian wives and fiancées of American servicemen went to the USA during and at the end of the war. (Australian War Memorial)

The maltreatment was caused by several factors. Japan was not a party to the 1929 Geneva Convention governing the protection of prisoners of war. Japanese troops were taught that it was a disgrace to surrender and those who surrendered were expected to commit suicide. Brutal physical punishment was part of discipline in the Japanese army. The thousands of Allied prisoners could expect no mercy, but at the same time they offered the Japanese a ready-made slave-labor force for the construction of military installations across the occupied area. Even if the Japanese had been inclined to provide

adequate food, it was in short supply as Allied submarine and air attacks decimated Japanese shipping. Furthermore, the countries of southeast Asia were subject to malaria and other deadly tropical diseases. None of this, however, excuses the sadistic treatment meted out by Japanese and Korean guards or the members of the Kempeitai. Even Red Cross parcels destined for the prisoners were stolen by the Japanese.

Treatment varied between areas. In April 1942, 78,000 Americans and Filipinos, already starving and weak from malaria, surrendered at Bataan. They were forced to march, beaten, clubbed, and bayoneted, with little or no food, 60 miles (100 km) to a prisoner-of-war camp. Between 7,000 and 10,000 died or were killed during the "Bataan Death March." During the war, a total of 25,600 Americans were held in Japanese prisoner-of-war camps; 10,600, or nearly

Allied prisoners of war building a bridge on the Burma–Thailand railroad in early 1943. More than 60,000 Australian, British, and Dutch prisoners of war worked on the railroad as slave laborers in appalling conditions on a starvation diet, and about 12,000 died, or one for every railway sleeper. (Australian War Memorial)

45 percent, died, most of starvation and disease. Australian prisoners, captured in Singapore, Java, Ambon, Timor, and New Britain, numbered 22,000; more than 8,000 or nearly 36 percent died. Britain had the most prisoners, including 10,000 captured in Hong Kong and 45,000 in Singapore and Burma. They suffered similar mortality rates to the Australians. The best-known camp was at Changi on the island of Singapore. From there work parties were sent to various places in southeast Asia. The Sandakan-Ranau camp in North Borneo held 2,500 British and Australian prisoners in mid-1943. Only six Australians survived.

Many prisoners were sent to work in Japan, where they slaved in coal mines, shipyards, and factories. They were transported in unmarked ships that were often attacked by Allied submarines. The Australians captured at Rabaul were sent to Japan, the officers and soldiers on separate ships. The *Montevideo*

Maru, with 849 soldiers and about 200 civilians, was torpedoed off Luzon and all were lost. Some prisoners sent to Manchuria suffered from hideous medical experiments at the Kwantung Army's Unit 731.

Japanese soldiers fought to the death rather than surrender, and there were thus fewer Japanese prisoners – about 5,000 in prisoner-of-war camps in the USA (mostly Koreans and Formosans) and a similar number in Australia. Japanese prisoners held at a camp at Cowra in Australia attempted a mass breakout in August 1944; 234 of the 1,104 prisoners were killed. The previous year, in a New Zealand camp, almost 50 Japanese prisoners died in a mutiny.

American and allied Filipino troops surrender to Japanese forces in Bataan, the Philippines. They soon joined the 75,000 American and Filipino prisoners of war (POWs) who were put on a 60 mile (97 km) forced march to Japanese prison camps. The so-called Bataan Death March lasted for a week and involved uninterrupted walking through tropical heat, with no food or water. Anyone who faltered--and many of those who tried to help them--were shot, bayoneted, beaten to death, or abandoned for dead. Somewhere between 6,000 to 18,000 POWs died or were murdered during the Death March, which was classified as a war crime in the post-war years.

Inevitably, Japanese attitudes to human life affected the Allies. Once Allied soldiers heard of Japanese atrocities, such as bayoneting prisoners, and saw evidence of cannibalism, such as occurred in New Guinea, they were less inclined to try to take prisoners.

Conclusion

The civilian populations of the nations involved in the war carried different burdens. Millions died in Japan and China, while few civilians in the USA died directly as a result of the war. The people whom the Japanese claimed they were liberating from European colonialism suffered cruelly at the hands of their liberators. In New Guinea and the Pacific Islands, the local natives were often treated harshly by the Japanese, with no suggestion that they might eventually become independent. It was truly a war between opposing races and cultures.

Gwen Harold Terasaki, an American in Japan

As an American married to a Japanese diplomat, Gwendolen Harold Terasaki lived in Japan during the worst days of the war, observing the life of ordinary Japanese women. Straddling two cultures, she sympathized with the plight of the Japanese people, but was conscious of the regime's militarism and brutality. Ultimately, like most people in Japan, her life became a struggle for survival.

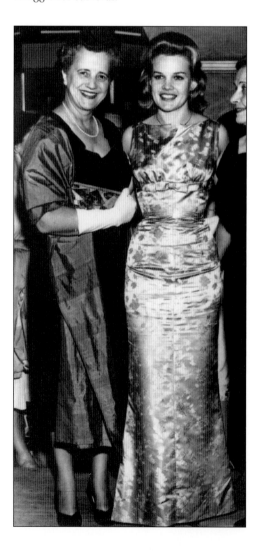

Gwen met her husband in 1930 when she visited Washington, DC, from her home town in Tennessee. Terasaki Hidenari, a diplomat at the Japanese Embassy, had attended university in the USA and spoke English well. They were married in November 1931, shortly before Terasaki returned to Tokyo; he was 31, his wife 23. Their next posting was at Shanghai where their daughter, Mariko, was born. Both Gwen and her husband were disturbed by the actions of Japanese troops in China. Hidenari (called Terry by Gwen) was in a difficult position. He was opposed to the Japanese militarists, but tried to serve his country loyally as a diplomat. They had further postings to Havana and Peking before returning to Washington in March 1941, where he was involved in diplomatic efforts to avert war between the USA and Japan.

On the outbreak of war, the Terasakis and other diplomats were interned with their families at Homestead Hotel, Hot Springs, Virginia. In June 1942 they sailed in a Swedish ship for Lourenço Marques, in Mozambique, where they transferred to a Japanese ship and reached Yokohama in mid-August.

In wartime Japan, Gwen noticed that people were looking at her clothes, and she packed away her nicest clothes for the duration, spending the war years "in slacks, sweaters, and skirts." Later, "as fuel became a thing of the past," she wore the "regulation *monpe*, a Japanese-type pantaloon which made up for its ugliness by being warm and practical."

In 1957 Gwen Terasaki (left) published *Bridge to the Sun* describing her wartime experiences in Japan. A movie based on the book, starring Carrol Baker and James Shigeta, had its premiere in her hometown, Johnson City, Tennessee, in 1961. Some critics at the time accused the film of being anti-American. (Archives of Appalachia)

Initially, Gwen lived in an apartment in Tokyo and became involved in the daily round of trying to keep a home. Against regulations, she baked a cake using her gas oven; their gas was cut off and thereafter she used a charcoal cooker. She described standing in line "for two or three hours for a few pieces of fish or a bunch of carrots," and noted that the "repeated air-raid drills also took up a large part of the day when they were called." Pregnant women were given priority for rations, and one day she witnessed "a pitiful but amusing incident" in the ration line.

A "pregnant" woman went to the head of the line and, after receiving her rations, started to walk off when out slipped a cushion from under her obi (sash). The other ladies sent up a howl and the poor woman broke into tears, explaining that besides seven small children to care for she had her mother-in-law, who was ninety, on her hands.

Like everyone, Gwen purchased food on the black market and once bought a small bunch of bananas for her daughter – the last bananas they were to eat until 1949. The Japanese used small round briquettes made from coal dust for heating, as they lasted longer than charcoal. One day a man told Gwen that he would sell them to her cheaper as they has just been made and were still wet. "He said that if I would lay them in the sun till they dried I could store them away. Feeling very proud of myself, I promptly took the whole lot, and the maid and I painstakingly arranged them in the sun. When they were dried out they crumbled – they were only blackened mud."

Early in 1944 the Terasakis moved to Odawara, near Sagami Bay, about three hours by rail from Tokyo. Despite the deteriorating war situation, only victories were broadcast on the radio. Gwen observed that this "involved such obvious contradictions that even the more simple-minded listeners became doubtful. Everyone who could think at all realized that the country was in a more and more desperate state, its back to the wall."

Boys of 10 and 12 were unloading the freight from trains, while children "were employed in all kinds of factory work from clothes-making to riveting airplane parts together; they were mobilized through their schools and taken to their jobs by the teachers."

As an Allied invasion force might land in the Odawara area, late in 1944 the Terasakis moved farther along the coast. There they endured a bitterly cold winter, foraging for sticks and pine cones for fuel. A small ration of horsemeat in January was particularly welcome when Terry became ill (he had a heart condition). Still worried about an Allied invasion, Terry wanted to move his family inland, but the bombing of Tokyo in March 1945 had sent thousands of homeless people searching for shelter and he had difficulty finding accommodation. Eventually a friend offered them his little summerhouse in the mountains above Suwa City, 75 miles (120 km) inland.

In their new home, food was an even more acute problem. They planted turnips, radishes, and beans, but the crops were pitifully small. Often the rice ration was delayed by up to 10 days, and they then had to forage for something to fill in. The three of them were growing weaker, and Mariko came down with dengue fever.

The authorities demanded more work. Resin from pines trees was used to manufacture fuel for aircraft, and each family in the countryside was required to extract a certain amount and turn it over to the local assembly. Called to that duty, Terry and his daughter collected the smallest quantity of resin of any family in the neighborhood. Gwen wrote: "Terry had always been opposed to the whole idea of a *kamikaze* corps, saying that if a country had to use such methods to continue, it should give up. The pine-tree tapping for fuel also depressed him, and he kept muttering, 'how long, how long.'"

All were suffering from malnutrition, and Gwen found that they had no energy beyond that needed to prepare their rice and keep the house and themselves clean. "My finger nails were almost gone," she wrote, "and I had to bandage my fingers to keep blood from getting on everything I touched."

One day she received as a gift Dickens' novel *A Tale of Two Cities*, about the French Revolution. Reflecting on her own situation, she now understood

the terror of people forced to eke out their everyday existence against a backdrop of chaos … The newspapers carried only victory stories and such headlines as, "Japan girds herself to give a knockout blow," but there were few people who did not know that Japan was almost at the end of the road. We discussed this with no one, as the kempei tai *had agents everywhere and people were being questioned every day. Some of them were being sent to prison.*

When Terry became ill again, Gwen, dizzy with malnutrition, was almost too weak to fetch the doctor. Then came news of the "strange bombing of Hiroshima." Gwen thought "that Japan would fight until the entire country was destroyed, the Japanese people broken and almost extinct." Terry disagreed, insisting "that among the Japanese statesmen there were realists who had a true love of country and the welfare of the people at heart." They learned of Russia's declaration of war, and that the Emperor would be broadcasting next morning. As a foreigner, Gwen decided not to accompany Terry and Mariko to the home where they had been ordered to assemble. On his return he told her that everyone was weeping, but when the Emperor stopped speaking, "Silently the old men, the women, and their children, rose and bowed to each other and without any sound each went along the path leading to his own house."

"Merrily, I put on earrings," wrote Gwen, "Mako [Mariko] wore a white dress and Terry donned a red tie. The war was over. White clothing had been forbidden during the war because it was too easily seen from the air. When Mako put on white it was like a ship turning on lights again after running blacked-out since 1941." But everyone else was apprehensive about the arrival of the Americans. One man asked Terry whether they would all be required to bow to the American soldiers. "If so," Terry replied, "I shall be the first Japanese to crack my forehead on the pavement. After all the Chinese in Shanghai and Peking that I have seen forced to kowtow before the Japanese soldiers, I hope to do the same with dignity."

During the occupation, Terry became an adviser to the Emperor. In 1949, concerned about Mariko's education, and with Terry's encouragement, Gwen and her daughter went to the USA, living in Gwen's home town. She planned to return to Japan, but on the outbreak of the Korean War, Terry advised her to wait. Then came news that he had died.

Mariko graduated from university, married an American lawyer, and had four children. Politically active, in 1976 she was elected to the Executive Committee of the Democratic National Committee, devoting herself to issues including the arms race, war and peace, racial and sexual equality, and political reform. Because of her husband's position, Gwen's experiences were not as tough as those endured by many. But, as she described them through Western eyes, they provide a picture that underlines the burden of war on Japanese civilians.

Not necessarily to Japan's advantage

The Pacific War did not end with one final and crushing battlefield defeat. The Allied victory was the outcome of relentless pressure that squeezed the life out of Japan's capacity to continue, even though millions of soldiers and civilians still remained willing to die for the Emperor. The atomic bomb attacks on Hiroshima and Nagasaki and the Soviet declaration of war merely gave the Japanese government the opportunity to surrender.

By July 1945 Japan was under siege from all sides. American and British carriers were conducting strikes against the home islands. American submarines were in the Sea of Japan. Most of Japan's navy had been sunk, and its overseas forces were isolated and surrounded. At home, however, the Japanese army was rapidly forming new divisions to repel the expected American invasion. Soon it numbered about 2 million troops in 60 divisions. These were supported by 3,000 kamikaze planes (with carefully preserved fuel), 5,000 regular warplanes, 3,300 suicide boats and a National Volunteer Force with a potential strength of 28 million. But Japan was running low on the equipment, fuel, food, and other resources needed to continue the war.

American forces under General MacArthur planned to land on Kyushu on November 1 with a force of 13 divisions, to be followed on March 1, 1946 by a landing on Honshu, near Tokyo, with a force of 25 divisions. From signals intelligence the American commanders knew the strength of the Japanese forces on Kyushu and feared heavy casualties.

Meanwhile, the Allied leaders were meeting at Potsdam in Germany, where Harry Truman, who had become US President on Roosevelt's death on April 12, told the Soviet leader, Joseph Stalin, that the USA had an atomic bomb that would be dropped on Japan. The Soviet Union had promised to join the war three months after the end in Europe, but as a Japanese surrender became more likely, the Americans became less keen on a Soviet attack, although they could do little about it. On July 26, 1945 the Allies issued the Potsdam Declaration, promising the utter destruction of the Japanese homeland unless there was an unconditional surrender. On July 28 the Japanese rejected this demand.

On August 6 an American B-29, the *Enola Gay*, based at Tinian, dropped the "Little Boy" atomic bomb on the city of Hiroshima. Again the Americans asked for surrender, promising another attack. The Japanese hoped that the Soviet Union might assist in negotiations with the Americans. They received their answer on August 8, when the Soviet Union declared war. Next morning Soviet forces invaded Manchuria, just ahead of news of another atomic bomb being dropped on Nagasaki, killing 35,000.

The double shock of the atomic bombs and the Russian attack decided the issue. On the night of August 9, three of the six members of the Imperial Council agreed to surrender. The other three wanted to fight on. The Emperor tipped the balance and decided to surrender; next day the Japanese government announced that it would accept the Allied terms provided they did not prejudice the prerogatives of the Emperor. The USA responded that the Emperor should be subject to the authority of the Supreme Commander for the Allied Powers. Late on August 14, Japan informed the Allies that it had accepted the terms. That evening several army officers attempted a coup. If the War Minister, General Anami Korechika, had supported the coup it might have succeeded, but he committed suicide, as did other military leaders.

The aftermath of the atomic bomb attack on Hiroshima on August 6, 1945. Some 78,000 inhabitants were killed – slightly less than in the first firebomb attack on Tokyo. Many others, however, were to die from the effects; by August 1946 the casualty figure had reached 120,000. (AKG Berlin)

At noon on August 15, the Emperor broadcast his orders to cease hostilities. He made no mention of surrender, but said that the war had "developed not necessarily to Japan's advantage," and that the enemy had employed "a new and most cruel bomb." Japan had "resolved to pave the way for a grand peace for all the generations to come by enduring the unendurable and suffering what is insufferable." Across the remnants of the Empire, with only a few exceptions, the members of the Japanese armed forces faithfully obeyed the order to cease hostilities.

In Manchuria, however, the war continued briefly. Between April and August 1945 the Soviets had moved 750,000 men and 30 divisions from Europe to the Far East.

Under the command of Marshal Aleksandr Vasilevsky, they formed the Far East Command with some 1.5 million troops (80 divisions), 5,500 armored vehicles, and nearly 5,000 aircraft. The Japanese Kwantung Army in Manchuria had 24 divisions, but eight of these had been mobilized in the previous 10 days. Although they had 1 million troops, the Japanese were outnumbered, had inferior equipment, and had a lower level of training and morale.

Experienced in mechanized operations, the Soviet commanders conducted a rapid mobile war. They quickly overran Manchuria, taking Harbin on August 18 and Port Arthur on August 22. Some Japanese units had not heard the order to cease hostilities, but in any case the Soviets were determined to keep fighting to secure as much ground as possible. Further, the Soviets were planning to land on the northern Japanese island of Hokkaido in late August. Stalin halted them at the last minute, after

Soviet sailors hoist a Soviet flag on a hill above Port Arthur, lost during the Russo-Japanese War of 1904–1905 and recovered during the Soviet invasion of Manchuria in August 1945. The Soviet Union had several scores to settle with Japan, including the recovery of territories taken by the Japanese 40 years earlier. (AKG Berlin)

Truman forcefully rejected his proposal to accept the Japanese surrender in northern Hokkaido. The invasion would have gone ahead if the atomic bombs had not induced Japan to surrender; Japan would then have been divided between the Soviet Union and the other Allies, as happened in Germany and Korea.

About 600,000 Japanese and Koreans were taken prisoner by the Soviets and transported to Siberia, to be used as forced labor. Only 224,000 survived to return to Japan and Korea in 1949. The Russians claimed that they killed 83,737 Japanese; the unofficial Japanese figure was 21,000. Soviet losses were put at just over 8,000 men killed and 22,000 wounded.

At the end of World War I, the Germans had surrendered without their homeland being invaded, leading to suggestions that somehow they had not actually been defeated. Japan was not invaded but there could be no doubt about the defeat. That the

Americans were prepared to invade, supported by massive firepower, was an important factor among the considerations that led to Japan's surrender.

From the beginning of the Pacific War it was clear that the decisive factor would be the industrial power of the USA. In July 1945 the USA had 21,908 front-line aircraft in the Pacific; the Japanese had 4,100. After the war Admiral Nagano Osami, Chief of the Naval General Staff, told his interrogators: "If I were to give you one factor ... that led to your victory, I would give you the air force."

It was not until the last year of the war that the USA was able to deploy and utilize its full industrial power. As General Ushijima

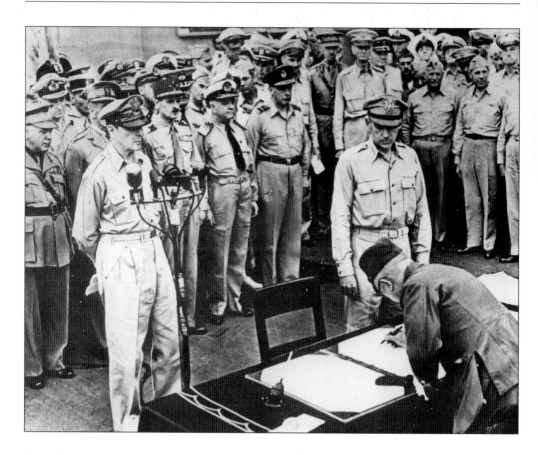

General MacArthur watches as a Japanese representative signs the surrender document on the battleship *Missouri* in Tokyo Bay on September 2, 1945. Admiral Nimitz signed on behalf of the USA with representatives, seen behind MacArthur, signing for the other Allies. (AKG Berlin)

Mitsuru, the Japanese commander on Okinawa, put it, "our strategy, tactics, and techniques were all used to the utmost and we fought valiantly. But it was as nothing before the material strength of the enemy." Prince Konoye, at one stage the Japanese Prime Minister and one of the Emperor's key advisers at the end of the war, said that "fundamentally the thing that brought about the determination to make peace was the prolonged bombing by the B-29s."

In view of the evidence that Japan did not have the economic strength to fight much beyond the end of 1945, arguments have continued as to whether the Americans needed to drop the atomic bombs. Various claims have been made about the extent of the casualties that the American forces would have suffered in the November invasion. But if the war had continued, thousands more Japanese civilians would have suffered both from American conventional air attacks and in the ground fighting. The fact that the Japanese Cabinet, after the shock of the atomic bombs, was still divided over whether to surrender indicates the role that the bombs played in terminating the war. For that, millions across Asia and the Pacific were grateful.

How the war transformed the Asia-Pacific

The Pacific War saw the deployment of huge forces across a vast geographic area, but it was still a relatively small war by comparison with the European theater – especially with respect to the numbers of soldiers mobilized for land operations. From a population of 194 million, the Soviet Union raised as many as 30 million troops, of whom more than 8 million were killed or died. Germany raised almost 18 million and more than 3 million died. British forces numbered almost 5.9 million with deaths exceeding 300,000 – mostly in Europe.

The eminent military historian John Keegan noted that "although the Japanese had mobilized 6 million men, five-sixths of those deployed outside the home islands had been stationed in China; the number committed to the fighting in the islands had perhaps not exceeded that which America had sent." Of the 29 US army and Marine divisions in the Pacific, only six army and four Marine divisions "were involved in regular periods of prolonged combat." By comparison, in the European theater in mid-1944 "300 German and satellite divisions confronted 300 Russian and seventy British and American divisions." The Japanese army still suffered heavily, incurring 1.4 million deaths. But this heavy loss of life was caused by the weight of firepower delivered by the Americans and the willingness of the Japanese to fight to the death, rather than by large-scale land battles.

Significantly, the Japanese navy also lost heavily – 400,000 deaths. The US navy lost 36,900 killed, mostly in the Pacific. These figures underline the maritime nature of the war. Japan began the war with a well-developed capacity for amphibious operations supported by carrier-based aircraft. As the war progressed, the US navy developed the concepts for carrier and amphibious operations to a new level. The US navy's carrier task forces became the most powerful elements of its fleet and this concept has continued through to the present time. In the Southwest Pacific Area, MacArthur used newly built jungle airstrips in the same way that Nimitz used his carriers, to provide air support for amphibious operations deep into enemy territory. The American naval operations were sustained by a huge fleet of supply ships – the fleet train. The naval war also showed the value of a competent and aggressively handled submarine force.

Allied naval and land-based air forces played a key role. For example, one assessment of the 2,728 Japanese ships sunk during the war reveals that 1,314 were sunk by Allied submarines, 123 by surface craft, 1,232 by direct or indirect air attack, and 46 by a combination of air and sea attack. Aircraft provided an invaluable means of transportation and resupply in a theater where land transport was extremely difficult and often impossible. Chinese and American forces in China were supplied by aircraft flying "the hump" from India. Transport aircraft moved troops in both the Burma and New Guinea campaigns. Troops were sustained by air resupply, often by parachute when landing fields were unavailable. Toward the end of the war, American strategic bombers alone brought Japan close to surrender, validating a concept that had produced less clear-cut results in Europe.

The atomic bomb attacks on Hiroshima and Nagasaki transformed warfare. As the American strategist Bernard Brodie wrote in 1946, "Thus far the chief purpose of our military establishment has been to win wars. From now on its chief purpose must be to avert them. It can have almost no other purpose." He was only partly right. Countries now tried to limit wars so that they would not escalate to the nuclear threshold.

Some of the skills learned in the Pacific War were employed in the limited wars of the following decades. For example, revolutionary forces in China, Malaya, Vietnam, and the Philippines exploited their guerrilla warfare expertise. The security forces deployed by the British Commonwealth in Malaya in the 1950s had learned their jungle warfare skills against the Japanese in Burma and New Guinea. The Allies had also learned how to provide logistic support in this difficult environment and to counteract the debilitating effects of tropical disease.

Although in 1945 the Allies deployed armies with up to a dozen divisions in Burma and the Philippines, they did not conduct the large-scale mechanized and armored operations that characterized the campaigns in Russia and northwest Europe and set the benchmark for the growth of mobile warfare in the following decades. Not much was modern about the grinding land battles of the Pacific War. But the use of carriers, amphibious operations, and air power in the Pacific set the stage for the further development of modern war. More generally, the war demonstrated the importance of cooperation between land, naval, and air forces.

Rebuilding Japan

At the end of the war, the immediate problem was to decide what to do with Japan, which could never again be allowed to conduct a war of aggression. Japan was a shattered society, but such societies can breed revolution and resentment of neighbors that can lead to future war. By the end of 1945, 13 million Japanese were unemployed. In the winter of 1945–46, the population was close to starvation. One survivor recalled, "Every last one of us was involved in the black market." A magistrate who nobly refused to become involved in the black market reputedly died of malnutrition.

General MacArthur, Supreme Commander for the Allied Powers, established his

Japanese servicemen arriving at Otake, Japan, from Sumatra after the war. Millions of soldiers and sailors had to be repatriated from overseas in Allied ships and demobilized. (Australian War Memorial)

headquarters in Tokyo and presided over an occupation force composed of mostly American troops with a small British Commonwealth force commanded by an Australian general. MacArthur set about establishing a Japanese government on largely Western democratic lines, and a new constitution came into effect in May 1947. Among its provisions were the renunciation of war forever as a sovereign right and the prohibition against maintaining military forces.

Determined to bring those responsible for the war to account, in 1946 the Allies established the International Tribunal for the Far East to try Japanese leaders with "crimes against peace." The charges included conspiracy to wage war and the waging of aggressive war, as well as conventional war crimes and "crimes against humanity." Some Japanese leaders, such as Prince Konoye, committed suicide before they could be arraigned. The Emperor, whom many thought should have been tried, was exempted from prosecution and from appearing as a witness, allegedly "in the best interests of all the Allied powers." The president of the court was an Australian judge, Sir William Webb. Two defendants died in custody and one was found mentally unfit to stand trial. All the others were found guilty of at least one charge. Seven, including Tojo, were hanged in 1948 and the remainder imprisoned.

Across southeast Asia, the Allies also conducted about 2,000 trials of those charged with murder, maltreatment of prisoners and civilians, and "crimes against humanity." About 3,000 of 5,700 defendants were found guilty and imprisoned; 920 were executed. In the Philippines, General Yamashita was charged with permitting atrocities against civilians during the defense of Manila. He claimed that he had no idea that the atrocities had occurred, but he was found guilty and hanged. General Homma was found guilty for permitting the Bataan Death March, despite claiming he had not heard of it, and was executed by firing squad.

The Allied occupation of Japan has been described as "wise and magnanimous." By September 1951, when the peace treaty was finally signed at San Francisco, the Japanese people hardly noticed the transition from the occupation administration to independence. At the same time, to help alleviate the fears of Australia and New Zealand about a possible resurgence of Japan as a military power, the USA signed a security treaty with those countries – the ANZUS Treaty. A year later the USA and Japan signed a security treaty, which continues to the present day. Sheltering behind the treaty, Japan grew into an economic powerhouse that contributed to the remarkable economic development of its former colonies and foes – China, Taiwan, South Korea, Hong Kong, and Singapore.

Reshaping the Asia-Pacific region

Although the Allied (mainly American) occupation of Japan enabled that country to be rebuilt as a democratic and eventually prosperous nation, elsewhere across the region the end of the war brought further turmoil and upheaval.

The most far-reaching was the civil war in China between Chiang Kai-shek's Nationalists and Mao Tse-tung's communists. The Nationalists had liberated much of southern China from the Japanese and were armed with US Lend-Lease equipment. In the north, the communists built up their army with captured Japanese weapons and with the assistance of the Soviet forces that flooded into Manchuria in August 1945. The war continued until 1949. On October 1, 1949 the Communist People's Republic of China was proclaimed at Peking, and by December the surviving Nationalist forces had withdrawn to Taiwan.

The Soviet invasion of northern Korea in August 1945 resulted in the division of Korea along the 38th parallel, and the establishment in the north of the communist regime under Kim Il-sung. The Republic of Korea was formed in the south under Syngman Rhee. In 1950 North Korean forces attacked the South, initiating the

Korean War. The 1953 armistice halted hostilities along the line of the original division, but Korea still remains divided.

In southeast Asia the revolutionary forces that had been formed during the Pacific War seized the opportunity to take over from their colonial masters. In Vietnam, for example, the communist nationalist leader Ho Chi Minh formed an independent government in August 1945. French troops reoccupied the country and were soon in battle with the Viet Minh. After their defeat at Dien Bien Phu in 1954 the French withdrew, leaving the country divided between the communist North and the Western-oriented South. The stage was set for the disastrous war involving the USA in the 1960s and 1970s that led to the unification of the country under communist rule.

In Indonesia, Sukarno proclaimed the formation of an independent republic. When British troops arrived, they were confronted by Indonesian forces. Dutch troops replaced the British, and for three years they struggled to regain control of the islands. In December 1949 the Netherlands formally surrendered sovereignty over Indonesia.

Unlike the French in Indochina and the Dutch in Indonesia, the USA had no desire to retain the Philippines, which formally became a republic in July 1946. One of the wartime guerrilla groups fighting the Japanese – the Hukbalahap, or Huks – was led by the communists, although it drew support from a wider group of peasant unions. Believing that they had been shut out of the new government, the Huks mounted a rebellion that continued until the mid-1950s.

The British government saw the trend of events and quickly gave Burma its independence. The new Burmese government soon faced a communist insurrection. Independence for India was not achieved until 1947, which saw the bloody and acrimonious partition of the country into mainly Hindu India and Muslim Pakistan. About half a million Muslims, Hindus, and Sikhs lost their lives during the massive relocation of the population.

Britain promised to grant independence to Malaya, but in 1948 the Malayan Communist Party launched an armed struggle using the Malayan Races Liberation Army (based on the wartime Malayan People's Anti-Japanese Army). Most of the insurgents were ethnic Chinese and hence the Malayan nationalists sided with the government. Malaya became independent in 1957. The Emergency, as it was known, officially ended in 1960, although some terrorist activity continued for many years.

The Pacific War was thus followed by 30 years of lesser (but still very bloody) wars across the Asia-Pacific region. They were driven by two imperatives – communism and decolonization – that came to prominence because of the Pacific War. At the end of that time the region had been transformed from that which existed before the onset of the Pacific War. In 1937 only Japan, China, and Thailand were independent countries and the Chinese Nationalist regime was not in full control of its country. The rest of the area was dominated by Britain, France, the Netherlands, the USA, and Australia. By 1975 China was a powerful united country under communist rule, except for Taiwan, already gaining strength as a separate economic entity. North and South Korea were in existence with the latter also becoming an economic power. Farther south and west, Vietnam, Laos, Cambodia, the Philippines, Brunei, Malaysia, Singapore, Indonesia, Papua New Guinea, Burma, Bangladesh, Sri Lanka, India, and Pakistan had become independent countries.

The Pacific War confirmed the involvement of the USA as a Pacific power. It committed large forces to the Korean and Vietnam wars, and has continued to base forces in Honshu, Okinawa, South Korea, and Guam. For many years it had air and naval forces in the Philippines. The mighty carrier battle groups of the Third and Seventh Fleets still patrol the waters of the Pacific. The USA's former enemy, Japan, is now one of its principal allies. Its former allies, the Soviet Union (now Russia) and

China, have been seen more as adversaries than as friends.

Japan's economic strength has given it friendly access to South Korea, China, southeast Asia, and Australia. But South Korea and China, and many people in the other countries, cannot forget Japan's wartime brutality. They are dismayed that some Japanese leaders (admittedly a minority) still refuse to acknowledge that their country fought an aggressive war and that their forces treated innocent civilians in an inhuman manner. The Pacific War might have transformed the region strategically, politically, and economically, but its shadow will hang over it for decades to come.

Glossary

amphibious A military operation involving the landing of assault troops on a shore from seaborne transport vehicles.

belligerent At war or seeking war; warlike.

clandestine Kept secret or hidden.

concession Something that is granted, yielded, offered, or given up, usually as part of an agreement or the settling of a claim.

counteroffensive An attack in force by troops who have been defending a position; a switch from a defensive position (defending against an attack) to an offensive one (going on the attack).

debilitating Becoming weak or feeble; wearing down.

expansionism The policy of expanding a nation's territory or its sphere of influence, often at the expense of other nations.

feudal The term for a political, economic, and social system in which common people work the land owned by a local warlord and make a living from it, in exchange for providing military and other services to the lord.

guerrilla A member of a small defensive force of irregular (not part of an official state army) and/or volunteer soldiers that makes surprise raids behind enemy lines.

imperial Relating to a country that has sovereignty, or governing control, over other countries or colonies; a term for a country that rules an empire or a country ruled by an emperor or empress.

intelligence The gathering of secret information for military or police purposes.

maneuver A planned and controlled tactical or strategic movement of troops, warships, aircraft, etc.; a skillful step toward some objective.

militarism The glorification of an aggressive, belligerent military spirit, especially in a society dominated by a military-based government; the policy of maintaining a strong military organization in aggressive preparedness for war.

mobilization The act of bringing something into readiness for immediate active service in war; the organizing of people (troops) and resources (vehicles, weapons, food supplies) for active service in war or an emergency effort.

nationalistic Demonstrating a devotion to one's country; excessive patriotism; the notion that national interests and security are more important than international considerations.

precipitate To cause to happen; to bring on or hasten.

provocation Something that causes irritation, anger, or resentment; something said or done that inspires or incites a strong, perhaps violent, response.

sanction A penalty (usually economic in nature) enforced by several nations in an attempt to persuade another nation to cease violating some standard of international law.

strategic Relating to a plan or course of action essential to effective military strategy; something designed to operate directly against the military or industrial installations of the enemy.

theater A scene of operations; in this case, a scene of military operations.

For More Information

National Military History Center
P.O. Box 1
Auburn, IN 46706
(260) 927-9144
Web site:
    http://www.militaryhistorycenter.org
The NMHC spotlights the service and
    sacrifice of America's military through a
    variety of museum units and major
    galleries dedicated to America's military
    in World War I, World War II, Korea,
    Vietnam, the Cold War, and today's
    War on Terror. The WWII Victory
    Museum is presently the centerpiece of
    this center, with other museums coming
    in the future.

National Museum of the Marine Corps
18900 Jefferson Davis Highway
Triangle, VA 22172
(877) 635-1775
Web site: http://www.usmcmuseum.com/
    index.asp
Opened in 2006, the National Museum of
    the Marine Corps is a tribute to U.S.
    Marines. Interactive exhibits surround
    visitors with irreplaceable artifacts and
    immerse them in the sights and sounds of
    Marines in action.

National Museum of the U.S. Navy
805 Kidder Breese Street SE
Washington Navy Yard, DC 20374-5060
(202) 433-4882
Web site: http://www.history.navy.mil/
    branches/org8-1.htm
Devoted to the display of naval artifacts,
    models, documents, and fine art, this
    museum chronicles the history of the
    United States Navy from the American
    Revolution to present-day conflicts.
    Interactive exhibits commemorate

wartime heroes and battles as well as
peacetime contributions in exploration,
diplomacy, navigation, and humanitarian
service.

National World War II Museum
945 Magazine Street
New Orleans, LA 70130
(504) 527-6012
Web site: http://www.ddaymuseum.org
Historian, author, and educator Dr. Stephen
    Ambrose founded the National World War
    II Museum Foundation in 1991. The
    museum, which opened in 2000,
    addresses all of the amphibious invasions
    of World War II, honoring the more than
    one million Americans who took part in
    this global conflict.

Pacific Aviation Museum
Hangar 37 on Ford Island
319 Lexington Boulevard
Honolulu HI 96818
(808) 441-1000
Web site:
    http://www.pacificaviationmuseum.org
This aviation museum is housed in the
    historic hangars that survived the attack
    on Pearl Harbor that started World War II
    for the United States.

U.S. Army Center of Military History
Fort Lesley J. McNair
Washington, DC 20319-5058
Web site: http://www.history.army.mil
The CMH is responsible for the appropriate
    use of history throughout the United
    States Army. Traditionally, this mission
    has meant recording the official history of
    the army in both peace and war, while
    advising the army staff on historical
    matters.

Veterans of Foreign Wars
National Headquarters
406 West 34th Street
Kansas City, MO 64111
(816) 756-3390
Web site: http://www.vfw.org
The Veterans of Foreign Wars of the United
States includes 2.2 million members in
approximately 8,100 posts worldwide. Its
mission is to "honor the dead by helping
the living" through veterans' services,
community service, national security, and
a strong national defense.

**World War II Valor in the Pacific National
Monument**
The USS *Arizona* Memorial at Pearl Harbor
1 Arizona Memorial Place
Honolulu, HI 96818

(808) 422-0561
Web site: http://www.nps.gov/valr/index.htm
The USS *Arizona* Memorial at Pearl Harbor
is "ground zero" for the United States'
involvement in World War II. The
USS *Arizona* serves as the final resting
place for the battleship's 1,177 crew
members who lost their lives on
December 7, 1941.

Web Sites

Due to the changing nature of Internet links,
Rosen Publishing has developed an online
list of Web sites related to the subject of this
book. This site is updated regularly. Please
use this link to access this list:

http://www.rosenlinks.com/wweh/paci

For Further Reading

Brooks, Victor. *Hell Is Upon Us: D-Day in the Pacific: Saipan to Guam, June–August 1944.* New York, NY: Da Capo Press, 2007.

DK Publishing. *World War II: The Definitive Visual History.* New York, NY: DK Publishing, 2009.

Gilbert, Sir Martin. *The Second World War: A Complete History.* New York, NY: Holt Paperbacks, 2004.

Holmes, Richard. *World War II in Photographs.* London, England: Seven Oaks, 2008.

Hopkins, William B. *The Pacific War: The Strategy, Politics, and Players that Won the War.* Minneapolis, MN: Zenith Press, 2009.

Keegan, John, ed. *Collins Atlas of World War II.* New York, NY: Collins, 2006.

Keegan, John. *The Second World War.* New York, NY: Penguin, 2005.

Kennedy, David M., ed. *The Library of Congress World War II Companion.* New York, NY: Simon & Schuster, 2007.

Marston, Daniel. *The Pacific War Companion: From Pearl Harbor to Hiroshima.* Oxford, England: Osprey Publishing, 2007.

Miller, Donald L. *D-Days in the Pacific.* New York, NY: Simon & Schuster, 2005.

A New Illustrated History of World War II: Rare and Unseen Photographs 1939–1945. Newton Abbot, England: David & Charles, 2005.

Stolley, Richard B. *Life: World War II: History's Greatest Conflict in Pictures.* New York, NY: Bulfinch, 2005.

Ward, Geoffrey C., and Ken Burns. *The War: An Intimate History, 1941–1945.* New York, NY: Knopf, 2007.

Weinberg, Gerhard L. *A World at Arms: A Global History of World War II.* Second edition. New York, NY: Cambridge University Press, 2005.

Bibliography

Official histories

Craven, W., and Cate, J. *The Army Air Forces in World War II*, 7 volumes, Chicago, 1948–58.

Kirby, S. W. et al. *The War Against Japan*, 5 volumes, London, 1957–69.

Long, G., ed. *Australia in the War of 1939–1945*, 22 volumes, Canberra, 1952–77.

Morison, S. E. *United States Naval Operations in World War II*, 15 volumes, Boston, 1947–62.

US Army. *United States Army in World War II, The War in the Pacific*, 11 volumes, Washington, 1948–63.

US Army. *United States Army in World War II, The China–Burma–India Theater*, 3 volumes, Washington, 1953–59.

US Marine Corps. *History of the US Marine Corps Operations in World War II*, 5 volumes, Washington, 1956–71.

Secondary sources

Allen, L. *Burma: The Longest War 1941–45*, London, 1984.

Allen, T. B., and N. Polmar. *Code-Name Downfall: The Secret Plan to Invade Japan and Why Truman Dropped the Bomb*, New York, 1995.

Bix, H. P. *Hirohito and the Making of Modern Japan*, New York, 2000.

Blair, C. *Silent Victory: The US Submarine War against Japan*, Philadelphia, 1975.

Callahan, R. *Burma, 1942–1945*, London, 1978.

Collier, B. *The War in the Far East 1941–1945*, London, 1969.

Daw, G. *Prisoners of the Japanese: POWs of World War II in the Pacific*, New York, 1986.

Dower, J. W. *War Without Mercy: Race and Power in the Pacific War*, New York, 1986.

Drea, E. J. *MacArthur's ULTRA: Codebreaking and the War Against Japan, 1942–1945*, Lawrence, KS, 1992.

Dull, P. S. *A Battle History of the Imperial Japanese Navy (1941–1945)*, Annapolis, 1978.

Feis, H. *The Road to Pearl Harbor: The Coming of the War between the US and Japan*, Princeton, 1963.

Frank, R. *Guadalcanal: The Definitive Account of the Landmark Battle*, New York, 1990.

Fuchida, M., and O. Masatake. *Midway: The Battle that Doomed Japan*, Annapolis, 1955.

Gailey, H. A. *The War in the Pacific: From Pearl Harbor to Tokyo Bay*, Novata, CA, 1995.

Horner, D. M. *Blamey: The Commander-in-Chief*, Sydney, 1999.

Horner, D. M. *High Command: Australia and Allied Strategy 1939–1945*, Sydney, 1982.

Ienaga, S. *The Pacific War: World War II and the Japanese, 1931–1945*, New York, 1978.

Ike, N., ed. *Japan's Decision for War: Records of the 1941 Policy Conferences*, Stanford, CA, 1967.

James, D. C. *The Years of MacArthur, Volume II, 1941–1945*, Boston, 1975.

Kirby, S. W. *Singapore: The Chain of Disaster*, New York, 1971.

Layton, E. T. *"And I Was There": Pearl Harbor and Midway – Breaking the Secrets*, New York, 1985.

MacArthur, D. *Reminiscences*, Greenwich, CT, 1965.

Potter, E. B. *Bull Halsey*, Annapolis, 1985.

Potter, E. B. *Nimitz*, Annapolis, 1976.

Prange, G. W. *Miracle at Midway*, New York, 1982.

Prange, G. W., D. M. Goldstein, and K. V. Dilon. *At Dawn We Slept: The Untold Story of Pearl Harbor*, New York, 1981.

Reynolds, C. G. *War in the Pacific*, New York, 1990.

Slim, W. J. *Defeat into Victory*,
    London, 1956.
Spector, R. H. *Eagle Against the Sun:
    The American War with Japan*, New
    York, 1985.
Thorne, C. *Allies of a Kind: The United States,
    Britain and the War against Japan,
    1941–1945*, New York, 1978.
Thorne, C. *The Issue of War: States, Societies
    and the Far Eastern Conflict of 1941–1945*,
    London, 1985.
Toland, J. *The Rising Sun: The Decline and
    Fall of the Japanese Empire 1936–1945*,
    London, 1971.

Tuchman, B. W. *Stilwell and the American
    Experience in China, 1911–1945*, New
    York, 1970.
Vat, D. van der. *The Pacific Campaign: The
    US–Japanese Naval War 1941–1945*, New
    York, 1991.
Willmott, H. P. *Empires in the Balance:
    Japanese and Allied Pacific Strategies to April
    1942*, Annapolis, 1982.
Willmott, H. P. *The Barrier and the Javelin:
    Japanese and Allied Strategies, February to
    June 1942*, Annapolis, 1983.
Willmott, H. P. *The Second World War in the
    East*, London, 1999.

Index

About the Authors

Professor Robert O'Neill is the Series Editor of the
Essential Histories. His wealth of knowledge and
expertise shapes the series content and provides up-to-
the-minute research and theory. Born in 1936 an
Australian citizen, he served in the Australian Army,
earned a Ph.D from Oxford, and has held a number of
eminent positions in history circles, including
Chichele Professor of the History of War at All Souls
College, Oxford, and Chairman of the Board of the
Imperial War Museum and the Council of the
International Institute for Strategic Studies, London.
He is the author of many books including works on
the German army and the Nazi Party, and the Korean
and Vietnam wars. Now retired from Oxford and based
in Australia, he is the Director of the Lowy Institute
for International Policy and Planning Director of the
US Studies Centre at the University of Sydney.

David Horner is the professor of Australian defense
history at the Strategic and Defence Studies Centre,
Australian University, Canberra. A graduate of the
Royal Military College, Duntroon, who served as an
infantry platoon commander in South Vietnam,
Colonel Horner is the author of more than twenty
books on military history and defense.